CONSTRUCTION INTO DESIGN

CONSTRUCTION INTO DESIGN

The influence of new methods of construction on
architectural design 1690–1990

James Strike

Butterworth Architecture
An imprint of Butterworth-Heinemann Ltd
Linacre House, Jordan Hill, Oxford OX2 8DP

 PART OF REED INTERNATIONAL BOOKS

OXFORD   LONDON   BOSTON
MUNICH   NEW DELHI   SINGAPORE   SYDNEY
TOKYO   TORONTO   WELLINGTON

First published 1991

British Library Cataloguing in Publication Data
Strike, James
    Construction into design: The influence of new
    methods of construction on architectural design
    1690–1990.
    I. Title
    721

ISBN 0 7506 1229 0

Library of Congress Cataloguing in Publication Data
Strike, James.
    Construction into design : the influence of new methods of
    construction on architectural design, 1690–1990/James Strike.
        p.   cm.
    Includes bibliographical references and index.
    ISBN 0 7506 1229 0
    1. Architecture–Technological innovations.   2.Architecture,
    Modern–History.   3. Construction industry–Technological
    innovations–Influence.   I. Title.
    NA2543.T43S7   1991
    721'.09'03–dc20   91-21763
                                                           CIP

Composition by Genesis Typesetting, Laser Quay, Rochester, Kent
Printed and bound in Great Britain by Butler and Tanner, Frome, Somerset

Contents

Preface

I have always been interested in how things are put together and how they work. I still have my large box of Meccano and I recall the pleasure of repairing the fine mechanism of our grandfather clock. I spent hours pursuing the patterns and construction in Bach's music, measuring the gradation of the stalks and stems in plants, and trying to visualize the little blobs of structural force squeezing down through the church columns. I wondered why such things fascinated me and I looked for a reasoned connection between their construction and my emotional response. I suppose that I was looking for some form of ultimate equation.

I was invited in 1980 to take up a tutorial post at the Kingston School of Architecture where again I found myself faced with similar questions. By this time my views were less simplistic but the issues remained equally fundamental. First, how can the student learn everything there is to know about building construction; second, how does the student choose a particular set of details from the endless number of possibilities and options that are now available? To the trained designer it may seem instinctive, but this intuitive response does not come naturally to the student. I explored certain hypotheses to establish some principles, I prepared a series of lectures on isolated aspects and discussed the problems with my peer group. Principles such as keeping out the rain, keeping the inhabitants comfortable and preventing the structure from falling down were calculable and straightforward. What fascinated me was how to set up principles which went beyond these scientific issues, principles which encompassed both the calculable issues and the emotional response, principles which considered construction as architecture, which realized the relationship inherent in the scientific issues as well as the important aspect of the designer's intention to create a coherent object with a specific image.

The debate developed at the summer conferences organized by the Institute of Advanced Architectural Studies of York University, and these meetings of like-minded tutors eventually led to my postgraduate thesis *The Influence of New Materials and New Methods of Construction on Architectural Design, 1700–1970* (IAAS, York University, 1988).

I believe that one of the most fruitful ways of understanding the connection between construction and design is to trace the way by which materials and forms of construction have evolved through history. It is through this evolution that we see the change in the appearance of buildings and the eventual recognition of building types.

The aim of this book is to develop this understanding. Although it is primarily intended for students of architecture, engineering and building, it will also serve as a useful stimulant and format of criticism for practitioners involved in the design process, and a source of reference for anyone concerned with the history of buildings.

J.S.

Acknowledgements

To the following who, each in their own way, have helped towards the material, the criticism and the preparation of this book.

John Adams
Tim Bell
Dennis Berry
Michael Blackstock
Tim Clark
Jonathan Coad
John Fiddler
Brian Gauld
Godfrey Golzen
Peter Jacob
Stephanie Leitch
Dick Linzey
Howard Martin
Edward Mills
Michael Rowley
John Savage
Caryl Stanley
Stuart Sutcliffe
Douglass Wise
Paul Woodfeild
Bastiaan Valkenburg

Special thanks to my wife Sarah and my sons Tom and Edward for their patience, encouragement and assistance.

Introduction

This book explores the events and developments within the construction industry that have changed the process of manufacturing buildings, leading to a change in the composition and appearance of buildings. It examines how this has led, often slowly, to a change in architectural design and, eventually, in the attitude of designers and the characteristics of design theories.

The construction industry is considered in its widest sense, its whole infrastructure, not only the materials and people on the building site, but also the companies that quarry the raw materials, the transport companies, the processing and manufacturing companies that produce composite building materials and standardized units, the architects and engineers who design the buildings, the teams in construction management and cost control, the finance companies that inject capital and speculate through property, and the government bodies that affect the industry. The resulting amalgam is not a static entity but an active and changing force responding to the economic, political and social aspirations of society.

It is through the construction industry that clients and architects seek not only to satisfy their material needs but also to fulfil other aspirations. John Ruskins describes the dual requirement for a building[1]:

> The practical duty divides itself into two branches, – acting and talking: – acting, as to defend us from weather or violence; talking, as the duty of monuments or tombs, to record facts and express feelings.

Architects in the design process need to raise building construction above the singularly physical solution to a higher mental plane which brings together the intellectual and aesthetic considerations with the physical requirements. The influential structural engineer Pier Luigi Nervi referred to this synthesis in the building process[2]:

2 CONSTRUCTION INTO DESIGN

Construction is by far the oldest and most important of the human activities. It springs from the material needs of the individual and society, but in satisfying people's needs it broadens to express their most spontaneous and deep feelings. Construction gathers in a unique synthesis the elements of manual labour, industrial organization, scientific theory, aesthetic sensibility and great economic interests. Construction creates our physical environment, and this exercises a silent but deep educational influence on each one of us.

Through the fabric of the building the architect proves the design solution and expresses the physical and emotional issues inherent in the specific project.

The design solution emerges from a complex interaction between the numerous issues which arise during the design process, and inevitably involves the selection of priorities amid conflicting influences. These include such diverse factors as finance, social attitudes, history, politics, manpower, materials, techniques, human expectations and emotions. From within this complex web the architect strives to design and construct a fabric which prudently realizes the design aspirations of the project. All these issues affect the appearance and aesthetic quality of the final building, some more directly than others. While the numerous factors are all interrelated, they can be divided into two recognizable groups. One group relates to the actual process of constructing buildings – for example materials, structure and technique. The other group relates to the contextual and externally applied issues such as town planning, sociology, context and historical precedence.

It is interesting to observe that, historically, the greater part of architectural writing about design and theory has dealt with the external and contextual issues; much less has been written on the influence which the process and activity of constructing buildings has had on architectural design. Architectural writing up to the nineteenth century can be divided into those texts which dealt with the classical building types, their correct proportion, decoration and style, and those which acted as practical manuals for the correct use of materials and accepted methods of construction. There is little evidence to show that the two were related. There are examples, such as Palladio's *Quattro Libri dell'Architettura* [3], which cover both aspects in the same series, but even here 'the preparation of the materials, and when prepared, how, and in what manner they ought to be put to use' [4] is dealt with in Book One, and 'the quality of the fabricks that are suitable to the different ranks of men' [5] is written about and illustrated separately in Books Two to Four. It was not until the effects of the industrial revolution began to show in the buildings and landscape of the early nineteenth century that criticism of the effect that construction was having on people's taste began to emerge. Much of this debate is referred to in this book.

Auguste Choisy, writing at the end of the nineteenth century, recognized that construction was an important ingredient of good architecture. His *Histoire de l'Architecture* [6], which covers the whole spectrum of architecture from the Greeks up to the nineteenth century, stresses the need to use the authentic method of construction for each building type, as this would lead logically to the correct architecture. This is interesting as it accepts a relationship between construction and architecture, but one which is inevitable and beyond the intervention or control of the architect [7]. This sense of constructional destiny became the central theme of the numerous manifestos produced during the first quarter of the twentieth century, manifestos written by fundamentalists who became known as the pioneers of the Modern Movement [8].

Although this book shares with Choisy, and the pioneers of the Modern Movement, a central interest in the influence of construction on buildings, it takes a less determinist attitude. It recognizes that not all innovations in construction have led to a change in architectural design, and that the roots of constructional innovations need to be seen within the context of the wide spectrum of issues which influence the building industry. Its aim is to explore and gain a deeper understanding of how, and to what extent, innovations within construction evolve and influence architectural design.

As a first step, it is necessary to consider how the numerous physical and emotional requirements of buildings interact. Historically, the designer and the constructor of a building were the same person, and so the interaction was natural. However, there has been a gradual move towards a separation of the two, with design consultants, architects and design engineers on the one hand, and constructors, administrators and builders on the other. The interaction between these two groups is now seen as a two-way process, a cross-fertilization. Design can lead construction and construction can lead design. This requires careful consideration. On the one hand, designers can modify and manipulate construction to achieve a particular effect – a notion which was repugnant to the rationalist pioneers of the Modern Movement at the beginning of this century, but which was exploited by such designers as Venturi in the early 1960s to achieve the historical metaphor and contextual irony which typified the Post-modern Movement [9]. On the other hand, construction can lead to the design solution; the rationale of the constructional technique can be seen as the generator which influences the design solution. In reality, most solutions are a particular mix of both, but the clarification does help to identify the specific route of this book: that is, its primary concern is with the influence of construction on architectural design rather than the manipulation of construction to achieve a particular reference. This restriction is aimed at focusing attention onto the aesthetics which are inherent within, and are generated by, construction.

It is now necessary to consider the ways in which the aesthetics, inherent within construction, influence design. There are two modes. The first is the way in which the designer selects and uses existing materials and methods of assembly, to create a building in which the artistry is achieved by a coherent and sensitive understanding of the characteristics of the materials used, and by an empathy for the nature and distinctiveness of the way in which the building is put together. The second mode is the way in which new materials and new methods of assembly gradually integrate into the building industry to provide the designer with an extended range of solutions, a greater number of design options. It is as if a new colour were added to the painter's palette; for example, try to imagine what would have happened if Titian had been provided with the additional option of a chemically based bright red pigment. A comparable event actually took place in the 1320s when the interiors of some churches were radically transformed upon the introduction of silver stain to produce a new yellow glass for the windows.

This study centres on the second mode. It thus explores and tests the following hypothesis:

The introduction of new materials and the formulation of new methods of construction within the building industry have led to changes in the practice and theory of architectural design.

The study plots a course through history to observe how changes in the building industry, particularly the introduction of new materials and the development of new constructional techniques, have led to a change in the design of buildings. It identifies those seminal buildings and events which, when considered in their chronological sequence, form an identifiable theme of development. It emphasizes the architectural significance of these transitions and is therefore an interpretation of history rather than an attempt to seek out new historical data. Each chapter centres on a particular thematic development and the chapters are arranged chronologically.

This strategy, important as it is as a method of identifying and understanding particular transitions, needs to be approached with caution. The selection of any route through history cannot take full account of the intricate and interweaving contemporary events with which it is surrounded. The written word is less able to cope with simultaneous events than music, which uses harmony and dissonance to develop several concurrent themes. Each of the selected themes needs, therefore, to be considered within the wider context of the whole study and the contemporary historical events which remain outside its scope.

The chronological chart in the Appendix (page 202) demonstrates the relationship and the overlapping nature of the themes.

The historical period of the survey is the three hundred years from 1690 to 1990. It thus begins at the dawn of the industrial revolution.

A brief consideration of the slow evolutionary changes which took place in building construction before the industrial revolution serves as a useful introduction to the historical survey.

The most important change within building construction during the seven hundred years leading up to the industrial revolution was the slow but relentless breaking down of local tradition. The isolated cells of building craft, steeped in local tradition and tied to the use of local materials, slowly loosened with the gradual improvements to transport and communication. Ideas began to influence people's actions and it slowly became feasible to transport alien building materials to satisfy these new aspirations. The inevitability which long-held traditions imposed on the appearance of the buildings within a locality still existed in 1700, although regional identity was beginning to be eroded, particularly by the landowners and the church who could afford the additional expense of importing ideas, materials and craftsmen into an area.

It is also necessary to recognize, within this pre-industrial period, a slow but relentless refinement of the medieval structural system of load-bearing masonry. This evolutionary process changed the natural architectural grammar from the small, dark, thick-walled cell buildings of the Saxon churches to the lofty, delicate and structurally balanced vaults of the thirteenth-century French cathedrals and to the vast structural brick domes of fifteenth-century Italy. The industrial revolution stimulated a more rapid type of change.

1 Pioneers of the iron frame, 1690–1840

The aim of this book, identified in the introduction, is to examine the hypothesis that new materials and methods of construction lead to a change in architectural design. The first opportunity to explore this concept arises with the introduction of structural iron into buildings during the eighteenth century. This chapter identifies a series of buildings that demonstrate an innovative use of iron, and considers the extent to which this led to a change in the appearance of the buildings.

Before picking up this story, it is first necessary to set the scene with a profile of the iron industry at the close of the seventeenth century[1].

Iron had traditionally been produced in small and uneconomic quantities by smelting iron ore in charcoal fired furnaces. The process was labour intensive and became progressively more uneconomic as the forests were cut down for furnace fuel and shipbuilding so that timber became scarcer and more expensive. Output from charcoal furnaces was either used for wrought iron forged and hammered into the required objects, or poured into sand moulds to produce cast-iron shapes.

The term 'hammered iron' is used in this book to describe this early form of hand wrought iron; it thus distinguishes it from the form of wrought iron produced industrially from the 1780s.

The contemporary writer Isaac Ware describes the production of cast iron from the traditional charcoal burning ironworks in the Forest of Dean, Gloucestershire[2]:

> In casting of iron, there is a bed of sand before the mouth of the furnace, in which they hollow out a kind of moulds, according to the figure and size of the pieces they intend.

He refers to the poor quality of these castings[2]:

> . . . and the brittleness of cast iron is such, what whatever is made of it, is liable to that accident, and often from the effect of air holes will bust even at the fire.

These early forms of hammered or cast iron were traditionally used in several ways in buildings prior to the end of the seventeenth century. Hammered wrought iron was used for decorative iron balusters and railings. These became expensive and fashionable status symbols from the 1690s[3], particularly for formal entrance gates, railings, iron screens and arbours. One of the finest craftsmen in this type of work was Jean Tijou whose iron screens at Hampton Court demonstrate the refinement possible in hand-wrought ironwork (Figure 1.1). Although

Figure 1.1 Hammered wrought iron screen, Privy Garden, Hampton Court, London, 1693; Jean Tijou (photograph James Strike)

the fabrications were complete in themselves there is no evidence to suggest that they were used to support parts of buildings.

Cast iron was used to make cannons, ordnances and other objects, and members of considerable size could be cast by this time as is seen in the large memorial iron tomb slabs made as early as 1619[4].

An early use of cast iron related to buildings was the railings erected around St Paul's Cathedral, London in 1714 (Figure 1.2). Sir Christopher Wren disapproved of them[5]; they would have been an intrusion into contemporary ideas about the cathedral precinct, their design derived neither from the lacey appearance of hammered wrought iron nor from the stout solidity of real stone balusters. Lethaby, however, writing one hundred years later, commented[5]:

> I do not see how the railings could have been better, they are heavy and rather blunt as befits the situation and the material of which they are made.

For Lethaby there was no longer 'the shock of the new'; his comment reflects his interest in craft and materials.

Figure 1.2 Cast iron railings, St Paul's Cathedral, London, 1714; Sir Christopher Wren (photograph James Strike)

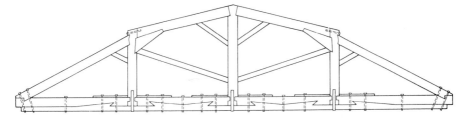

Figure 1.3 Timber truss with iron fixings, Sheldonian Theatre, Oxford, 1669; Sir Christopher Wren (reproduced from *Timber in Construction*, edited by John Sunley and Barbara Bedding, courtesy of the Timber Development Association)

Iron from the charcoal furnaces was used to make the fixing straps and brackets introduced during the seventeenth century to strengthen timber roof trusses[6]. Metal straps at the feet of king posts were used to 'truss up' the tie beam; together with other metal fixings, they contributed to an improvement in the structural efficiency of the truss. Sir Christopher Wren's roof trusses for the Sheldonian Theatre, Oxford, 1669, demonstrate how the use of iron fixings allowed the 21 metre span to be achieved using convenient lengths of timber (Figure 1.3). These structural improvements developed in a somewhat empirical manner[6] right up to 1820 when Thomas Tredgold published *Elementary Principles of Carpentry*, the first reference book on timber structures to be based on scientific knowledge[7].

Iron members were also built into masonry to strengthen the structure. An iron member was used as early as 1638 to support the masonry lintel of the brick furnace at Coalbrookdale, Shropshire. The natural limits of masonry construction were gradually extended with concealed iron cramps, cross-ties and reinforcing bars to allow the building of the large porticoes and colonnades of the Rationalist architecture of the eighteenth century[8]. As early as 1670 Claude Perrault, with Le Vau and Le Brun, relied on a considerable amount of iron reinforcement to achieve his Louvre Colonnades, Paris (Figures 1.4, 1.5). This constructional device became common practice during the eighteenth century, although recent restoration of some of these buildings has revealed that the structural principles of reinforcement were not always fully understood[9].

The concealed use of structural iron took on a more significant role in the building of St Paul's Cathedral, 1675–1710, where two heavy chains, forged in the ironworks at Lamberhurst in the forests of the Sussex and Kent border, were used to restrict the outward thrust of the inner dome of brickwork.

Figure 1.4 Louvre Colonnades, Paris, 1670; Claude Perrault (reproduced from *Cabinet du Roi*, courtesy of the British Architectural Library, RIBA, London)

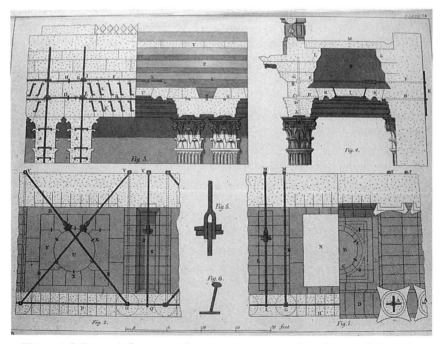

Figure 1.5 Iron reinforcement for masonry construction, Louvre Colonnades, Paris, 1670; Claude Perrault (reproduced from *The Mason's, Bricklayer's, Plasterer's and Decorator's Practical Guide*, Robert Robson, courtesy of Robin Wyatt library)

The development of iron for use as structural members in buildings needs to be seen as an integral part of the Industrial Revolution. Certain key issues need to be identified: the growth in coal mining, the increased production of iron, the development of new manufacturing techniques and the improvement of transport. Coal output in Britain in the early 1640s was 1.5 million tonnes per year, in 1770 it was 6 million tonnes, and by 1850 it had reached 50 million tonnes. Most relevant to this chapter is the growth of iron production. Output from the charcoal furnaces reached about 17 000 tones per year at the beginning of the eighteenth century. In 1709, Abraham Darby successfully developed an improved process of smelting iron using coke as a fuel; the process quickly became economic and by the 1740s production had overtaken output from the charcoal furnaces. By 1750 the new process was producing 30 000 tonnes of iron per year, in 1780 the first large commercial iron foundry had been opened at the Carron Works at Coalbrookdale in Shropshire, in 1794 Wilkinson introduced the more economic cupola blast furnace, and by 1800 production had increased to over 250 000 tonnes per year. Key events which stimulated improvements in manufacturing were the introduction of Kay's flying shuttle in 1733, Hargreave's Spinning Jenny in 1764–7, James Watt's steam engine in 1769, and the Reverend Edmund Cartwright's patents for the power loom taken out between 1785 and 1787. These led to a change from home-based craft production to a factory-based system of employment, causing a migration of workers from the countryside to the towns, with its social implications for the expanding population. The period from 1720 to 1830 saw the great canal system develop and between 1750 and 1820 great improvements were made to the roads of Britain such that, with the use of macadam (John Macadam 1756–1836), the travel time from York to London was reduced to 31 hours. It is against this background that the development and influence of iron in architecture needs to be considered.

An early structural use of cast iron was for the new waterworks at London Bridge in 1702. However, this was more of an industrial installation than an architectural edifice[10]. The water-powered pumps, constructed between the end piers of the river bridge, were designed by the engineer Sorocold and included great iron crankshafts with iron connecting rods over three metres in length and cast-iron pumping cylinders 225 mm in diameter.

The first use of cast iron as structural members in an architectural sense was in 1714 at the House of Commons. The House at that time sat in St Stephen's Chapel of the Palace of Westminster. Pugin and Rowlandson refer to Sir Christopher Wren's use of slender iron pillars to support the new galleries (Figure 1.6)[11]:

> . . . to the time of Queen Anne, in whose reign Sir Christopher Wren was employed to repair the building, and fit up its inside with galleries. . . . The House of Commons is plainly fitted up, and accommodated with galleries, supported by slender iron pillars, adorned with Corinthian capitals and sconces.

The new problem arose: how to make a visually acceptable connection between the slender iron shaft and the traditionally proportioned corinthian capital? The result shows an uncertain solution, confused between the visual language of classic detailing, flag poles, lanterns and structural iron. The choice of slender iron pillars was no doubt a pragmatic one to retain good sight lines across the chamber, but iron had not been used in this way before and there were no established rules for the designer. A comparison with the contemporary building of St Alfege Church, Greenwich, by Nicholas Hawksmoor suggests

Figure 1.6 Cast iron columns to the galleries, House of Commons, St Stephen's Chapel, Palace of Westminster, 1714; Sir Christopher Wren (reproduced from *The Microcosm of London*, Pugin and Rowlandson, courtesy of Bastiaan Valkenburg library)

Figure 1.7 Tapering timber supports for the balconies, St Alfege Church, Greenwich, London, 1711–14; Nicholas Hawksmoor (photograph Bastiaan Valkenburg)

that galleries were seen as part of the furniture and fittings within the interior of the building rather than as part of the structural body of the church. Hawksmoor clarified this distinction by his use of tapering 'chairleg' supports for the galleries (Figure 1.7).

It was not until 1752 that iron provided a direct contribution to the structure of a building. This was at the Cistercian Monastery of Santa Maria de Alcobaça in Portugal, where, for the reconstruction of the kitchens, eight cast-iron columns, tied together at the top with hammered iron strap beams, were used to support a massive stone chimney-hood over the large cooking hearth (Figure 1.8). Probably the iron columns were used not to produce an architectural effect but simply to allow wider access to the cooking spits. The columns were not thought worthy of mention by William Beckford when he wrote his florid description of the kitchen in 1794[12]:

> . . . the most distinguished temple of gluttony in all Europe . . . my eyes never beheld in any modern convent of France, Italy, or Germany, such an enormous space dedicated to culinary purposes . . .

He continues to describe the scene in detail without any reference to the iron columns. Beckford, for whom James Wyatt built Fonthill

Figure 1.8 Cast iron columns for the stone chimney hood, kitchen, Santa Maria d'Alcobaça Monastery, Portugal, 1752 (photograph Bastiaan Valkenburg)

Abbey, was a notable connoisseur and critic of architecture, yet the innovatory use of iron at Alcobaça was of no importance to him. It is also interesting to observe that an early drawing of the kitchen by Aldemira[13] depicts these slender 190 mm diameter iron columns as having the thickness of a structural stone member of sufficient bulk to take the massive weight. Even the eye of the artist was not at that time attuned to the new visual language of iron construction.

The cast-iron columns in the House of Commons in 1714 and at Alcobaça in 1752 are early and lonely examples of the use of iron in building. Abraham Darby had successfully smelted iron using coke fuel as early as 1709 and production of iron had more than doubled during the first half of the eighteenth century, yet iron was used remarkably little for building during this period. Taking England as an example, there are only a few structural uses of iron right up to the 1790s: principally, the columns to support the galleries at the House of Commons (1714), columns for the galleries at St Anne's Church Liverpool (1770–2), and the cast-iron structure for the 7.5 metre diameter glazed lanterns over the principal offices of John Soane's Bank of England (1792) (Figure 1.9)[14]. It was not until the 1790s that iron became accepted for structural members in building, and two events can be taken as being symptomatic of the reasons for the

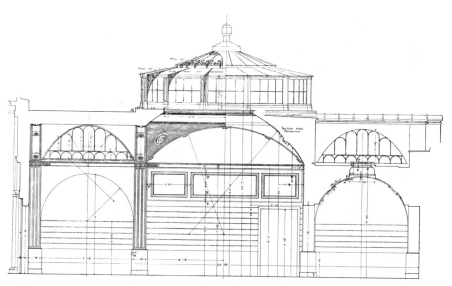

Figure 1.9 Cast-iron lantern, Stock Office, Bank of England, London, 1792; Sir John Soane (reproduced from *The Old Bank of England*, H. Rooksby Steele and F. R. Yerbury, courtesy of Bastiaan Valkenburg library)

change. First, the construction in 1777–9 of the Iron Bridge at Coalbrookdale helped to overcome the lack of confidence about the use of cast iron for structural members. Second, the destruction by fire of the Albion Flour Mill, London, in 1791 encouraged greater use of cast iron to achieve a fireproof construction.

The Iron Bridge over the River Severn at Coalbrookdale (Figure 1.10) represents a considerable move forward in the structural use of cast iron[15]. It was designed by Thomas Pritchard, an architect from Shrewsbury, in collaboration with the ironmaster John Wilkinson, and was built by Abraham Darby III using his Coalbrookdale ironworks to cast the members. The bridge is interesting not only for its daring use of iron to achieve the 30.5 metre span, but also for its proof that it was possible and practical to build using cast iron. Pritchard, Wilkinson and Darby were faced with a new problem; it was the first time that cast iron had been used for such a structure and there was therefore no proven set of construction details to use for the iron joints. Faced with this problem, they had to work out a new system of joints. Pritchard was the son of a carpenter-joiner and, in collaboration with Wilkinson and Darby, he worked out a system of construction using the known

Figure 1.10 Ironbridge, Coalbrookdale, Telford, Shropshire, 1777–9; Thomas Pritchard and John Wilkinson (photograph James Strike)

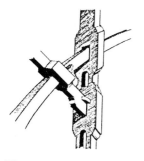

Figure 1.11 Construction joints, Ironbridge, Coalbrookdale, Telford, Shropshire, 1777–9; Thomas Pritchard and John Wilkinson (drawings by Pat Read for the Ironbridge Gorge Museum)

vocabulary of wedges and dovetails derived from detailing timber structures (Figure 1.11). The bridge therefore represents a transition between traditional timber construction and a new system of iron construction.

The burning of the Albion Flour Mill in 1791 brought to a head the need to reduce the fire risk which these timber floored buildings presented. There had been other serious fires in the recent past, notably the loss in 1781 of Arkwright's first mill buildings, together with the loss of the Théâtre du Palais Royal, Paris, in the same year, but none had such an impact as the destruction of this important mill situated in the industrial centre of London. The Albion Mill, designed by the architect Samuel Wyatt with the engineer James Rennie, was only five years old when it was completely gutted by fire and its loss forced the insurance company to impose prohibitive rates on all such timber structures. Fire fighting in the 1790s was almost ineffectual (it would be another 60 years before the introduction of the first Shand and Mason steam powered fire engine). The Phoenix Fire Office had been set up in 1680 but still covered only the City areas. There was little opportunity of obtaining alternative quotations.

The striving for less vulnerable mill buildings was encouraged by the mill owners who wanted to protect their assets, and also by the Philanthropic Movement with its concern for the conditions and safety of the mill workers. Hitherto the only way of producing fireproof floors had been to use masonry vaults, but these were disproportionately expensive for use in mill buildings as their weight prevented the construction of multiple storeys. Simple attempts were made to fireproof timber buildings with thin iron plates nailed to the underside of the timber boards and joists, but these were not very effective[16].

The gradual introduction of cast-iron members to replace timber columns, beams and floors can be traced through a series of mill buildings starting in the early 1790s.

The introduction of iron into the mill buildings did not in itself create a new architectural type. The form of the industrial mill had been established earlier by such buildings as John Lombe's Silk Mill at Derby of 1718–22, a 12 × 33 metre rectilinear masonry box containing five storeys of timber columns, beams and floors. The evolution of the mill buildings did, however, provide an opportunity to develop the structural system of the iron frame.

Iron had by this time been used to construct complete roof trusses; a significant example was in the rebuilding of the Théâtre du Palais Royal in Paris in 1786–90 by Victor Louis. An important step towards the construction of the iron frame was taken in 1792–3 in the building of the William Strutt Mill at Derby where, for the first time, cast-iron columns were used in place of timber to support the six floors inside the building. This building is also interesting for its early use of segmented brick arches spanning between the timber floor joists to provide a fireproof floor. The undersides of the floor joists were plastered, and the undersides of the timber plates which supported the brick arches were faced in sheet iron[17].

The next step forward was the building 1796–7 of the Benyon, Bage and Marshall Flax-spinning Mill at Ditherington new Shrewsbury (Figure 1.12). Cast iron was used not only for the columns but also for the beams to support the shallow brick floor arches. This construction of three rows of iron columns connected across by iron beams rises for five floors within the 12 × 55 metre enclosing masonry box to form what is recognized as one of the earliest examples of an iron frame. The beams used to span the 2.65 metres between the columns are no more than a vertical section of iron slightly splayed out towards the bottom to provide support for the shallow brick floor arches[18]. It is interesting to note that Charles Bage's commitment to cast iron was such that even the windows at the Ditherington Mill were cast in iron.

In 1797, William Strutt built the Belper Mill using a similar form of construction to that used at Ditherington but with the beam span increased to 3 metres. Here there are two rows of columns, giving an overall width to the mill of 9 metres.

The Salford Twist Mill by Messrs Phillips, Wood and Lee was built in 1799–1801 (Figure 1.13). Here the beam span is increased to 4.2 metres and the height of the building taken to seven floors. The beams designed by Boulton and Watt are similar to the section used by Bage

Figure 1.12 Interior, Benyon, Bage and Marshall Flax Spinning Mill, Ditherington, Shrewsbury, Shropshire, 1796–7; Charles Bage

for Ditherington but with the addition of a projecting toe at the base of
the splayed section to form a seating for the brick arches. There is
conjecture as to whether this beam or the slightly developed beam used
for the Holdsworth Mill at Glasgow of 1802 represents the first use of
the structural facility of the inverted 'T' section. The columns
manufactured by George Lee for the Salford Twist Mill (Figure 1.14)
are also interesting as they were the first to be cast as circular hollow
columns in place of the previously used solid cruciform section. These
columns are 165 mm diameter for the bottom two floors and 140 mm
diameter for the upper floors. While the internal iron frame structure
of the Salford Twist Mill follows the layout of the earlier timber
structures, it has now grown in its number of storeys and widened in
its spacing of the columns beyond that which could have reasonably
been built in timber. It is an iron frame construction, but still
contained within a masonry box.

Confidence in the use of iron was encouraged during the early
nineteenth century by structures other than the mills. The Halle du
Blé by J. F. Bélanger and F. Brunet was roofed by a 40 metre iron

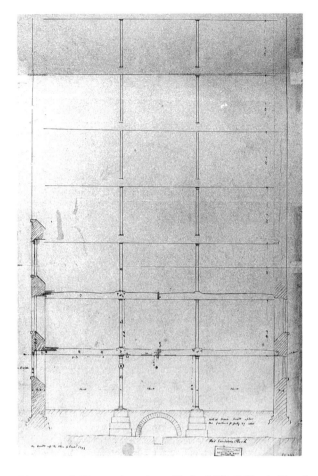

Figure 1.13 Plan and sections, Twist Mill, Salford, Manchester, 1799–1801; Lee and Boulton and Watt (courtesy of the Boulton and Watt Collection, Birmingham Central Reference Library)

dome in 1809–13[19]. The Tobacco Dock at Wapping on the Thames, by Daniel Alexander and John Rennie (1811–14), demonstrated how a kit of iron parts could be used to build up columns and spreaders to support the large timber trusses (Figure 1.15), and in 1818 structural iron was given royal approval through its use by John Nash for the structure of the dome of the central saloon of the Brighton Pavilion.

During the 1820s, a series of systematic investigations were carried out to determine the form and strength of cast-iron beams. Tredgold published a paper in 1824, Hodgkinson carried out investigations in

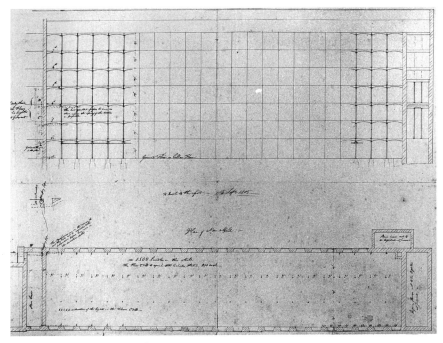

Figure 1.13 (*continued*)

1827 and Fairburn also carried out some practical experiments in the late 1820s. In 1830 Hodgkinson submitted an important paper to the Manchester Literary and Philosophical Society entitled *Theoretical and Experimental Research to Ascertain the Strength and Best Form of Cast Iron Beams* in which he demonstrated the potential of having a flange at both the top and bottom of the web. This brought much of the previously produced theoretical work[20] to a level where it could be practically applied in the development of the iron frame.

The advantages of using structural iron were thus adopted on a wider field. One of the earliest examples in a non-industrial building was in 1816 when Robert Smirke adopted a composite cast-iron structure with wrought-iron tie rods as a floor truss at Worthy Park[20]. This was followed in the early 1820s at the British Museum, again by Smirke, where heavyweight cast-iron girders over a metre deep were used for the floor of the King's Library.

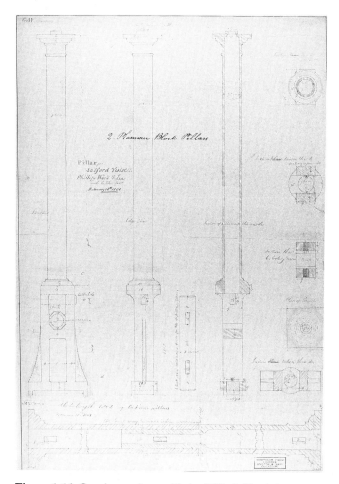

Figure 1.14 Cast-iron column, Twist Mill, Salford, Manchester, 1799–1801; Lee and Boulton and Watt (courtesy of the Boulton and Watt Collection, Birmingham Central Reference Library)

By the 1830s architects were familiar with these techniques. Decimus Burton showed his clear and confident use of the structural working of iron in the construction of the Old Charing Cross Hospital in 1830. The beams over the sick ward cast by Bramah and Sons, demonstrate the sort of complex castings which were used at this time (Figure 1.16).

By the 1830s, the Industrial Revolution was making a significant impact on all walks of life. The textile and dressmaking industry, for example, expanded eightfold between 1800 and 1852. With this

Figure 1.15 Cast-iron column and spreader, Tobacco Dock, Wapping, London, 1811–14; Daniel Alexander and John Rennie (photograph James Strike)

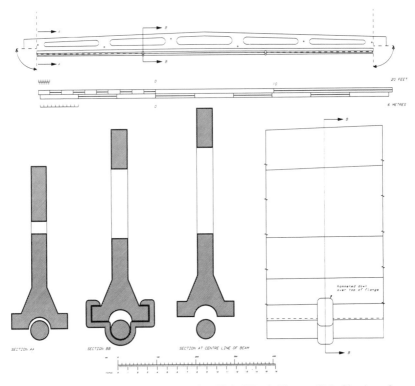

Figure 1.16 Cast-iron beams over the Sick Ward Floor, Old Charing Cross Hospital, The Strand, London, c.1830; Decimus Burton (survey drawing by Alan Fagan for English Heritage)

growth came the centralization of production, encouraged by the improvement of the roads and canals, the opening of the railways and the introduction of larger and improved industrial machinery[22]. Thomas Carlyle in *Signs of the Times*, written in 1829, emphasizes the impact of this new industrial growth[23]:

> Were we required to characterise this age of ours by a single epithet, we should be tempted to call it, not an Heroical, Devotional, Philosophical or Moral Age, but, above all others, the Mechanical Age. It is the Age of Machinery, in every outward and inward sense of that word.

The new cast-iron structures made it possible to construct the new large buildings to house the rows of new machines. The buildings were the 'outward sense' of the Mechanical Age.

William Fairburn took advantage of the new knowledge about structural iron to build larger and more economic mills for the

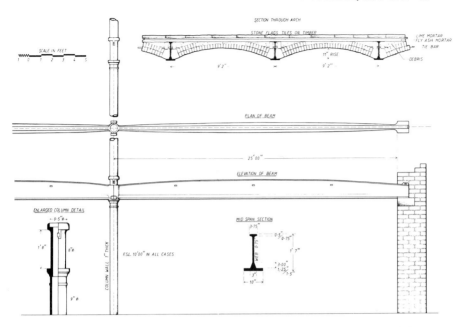

Figure 1.17 Cast-iron beam, Orrell Mill, Stockport, Manchester, 1834; William Fairburn (drawing by Ron Fitzgerald, Leeds Industrial Museum)

manufacturers. In 1834 he built the Orrell Mill at Stockport where the structural advantage of a flange at both the top and bottom of the beam was used for the first time to achieve a beam span of 7.25 metres (Figure 1.17). This arrangement at the Orrell Mill demonstrates the potential of the iron frame (Figure 1.17). It is primarily this form of construction which was used to build the numerous mill buildings of the 1840s.

It is difficult to determine the visual effect which these new large industrial buildings had on the landscape during the first half of the nineteenth century. Alexis de Tocqueville, in *Journeys to England and Ireland* of 1835, sets the scene by depicting the undulating landscape of Manchester[24]:

> Thirty or forty factories rise on the tops of the hills I have just described. Their six storeys tower up; their huge enclosures give notice from afar of the centralisation of industry. The wretched dwellings of the poor are scattered haphazard around them. Round them stretches land uncultivated but without the charm of rustic nature. . . . The land is given over to industry's use.

This upsurge in the construction of identical buildings in the industrial areas throughout the country must have contributed to the breakdown of regional identity in the appearance of buildings. The vernacular pattern of buildings, based on local materials, geology and climate[25], was being replaced by large identical buildings to serve industrial growth.

It is of no wonder that B. C. W. von Beuth, the Prussian Minister of Commerce, should be dispatched to England in 1823 to investigate this surge of industrial growth. He was impressed by what he saw[26]:

> . . . plenty of factories of eight and nine storeys with paper-thin walls, iron columns, and iron beams.

The size and construction of these buildings were new to him, and his use of the phrase 'paper-thin walls' implies that as early as 1823 the iron skeleton frames inside the mill buildings were already taking much of the structural loading which had previously been taken by thick external load-bearing masonry walls. Similarly, when B. C. W. von Beuth returned to England in 1826 he was accompanied by the architect Karl Friedrich Schinkel, who, in his diary, records page after page of concise technical data about the advanced state of industry in Britain[26].

It would appear that Beuth and Schinkel saw these industrial buildings not as the 'dark satanic mills' depicted by the contemporary poet William Blake[28] but as pioneering and technical constructions to serve the growth of industry. Schinkel's sketch of the mills (Figure 1.18) certainly portrays the impression that he saw them as powerful and modern buildings.

Although mill buildings stimulated the development of the iron frame, it was not in this form that the iron frame first broke free of its enclosing wall to stand on its own. One of the first occasions that this

Figure 1.18 Sketch of the industrial mills, *c*.1826; Karl Friedrich Schinkel

Figure 1.19 Fire Station Building, Naval Dockyard, Portsmouth, Hampshire, 1843 (photograph James Strike)

happened was in 1843 in the construction of the Fire Station Building at Portsmouth Naval Dockyard (Figure 1.19). This was built to hold up large water tanks, since removed, for fire fighting in the dockyard. The building demonstrates an understanding of the structural principles of iron construction, the casting of its separate parts, its jointing, and its visual expression as an iron frame standing on its own.

2 A new language from the use of iron and glass, 1810–1855

The previous chapter explored the evolution of iron construction through the building of the industrial mills. It established that this development began by replacing timber construction and went on to establish a new, larger and wider-spaced skeleton form of iron frame. While this facilitated the construction of larger mill buildings, and established that iron was a suitable material for building, it did not in itself create a new architectural language, nor create a new type of building.

This chapter follows a series of buildings and events which, through the use of iron and glass, did establish a new architectural language, one that was to emerge in the buildings of the 1850s. The result is clearly represented by the building of the Crystal Palace in 1851, where all of the various evolutionary issues came together into one clear and coherent architectural statement.

One of the earliest buildings in which the use of iron can be seen to have influenced its appearance was St George's Church, Everton, Liverpool (Figure 2.1). This church was designed by Thomas Rickman and John Cragg and was built using a cast-iron structure as early as 1812–14. While the structure retains the lines of ecclesiastic Gothic, the slenderness of its sections, particularly in the columns and roof trusses[1], shows that it is not built of stone but assembled from iron members. This new visual effect could not have existed in any previous church interior; its tenuous lines go beyond even the most refined of the late Gothic stone structures.

The conventional appearance of church buildings was still important, however, and St George's was encased in an external wall of stone. Nevertheless the interior is important for its early use of a large-scale prefabricated dry structure. All the pieces were made in the factory of John Cragg, taken to site by horse and cart, and bolted into position.

The Bishop of Chester referred to Thomas Rickman as 'a very ingenious and deserving man', and encouraged him to give evidence to the Church Commissioners on the value of this form of construction[2]. Although this interest may have related to economics, it shows that the church authorities did not wish to resist the new

Figure 2.1 St George's Church, Everton, Liverpool, 1812–14; Thomas Rickman and John Cragg (photograph James Austin)

tenuous appearance of the interior structure; perhaps they were more concerned with the correctness of the Gothic mouldings included in the cast-iron members.

During 1814–15, Rickman and Cragg built a second church in Liverpool. At St Michael in the Hamlet, Aigburth, they used the same construction and made use of many of the casting moulds used for St George's. The same prefabricated cast-iron structure was expressed internally, but here the iron structure was also partially expressed externally as it passed between the clerestory windows. Cast iron was also used as a cheap method of producing the 'imitation stone' finials, parapets and copings.

Another church which pursued this development was St Paul's, Southsea. Designed by Francis Goodwin and built in 1820–2, it used iron members for its fine Perpendicular nave structure and also for the elongated Perpendicular-style tracery windows. It was gutted in World War II and subsequently demolished[3].

The emergence of a new architectural language is continued through the large glass and iron horticultural hothouses constructed during the 1820s. In these buildings there was a less restrained attitude towards appearance and less need to use iron to reproduce historical architecture. Their evolution was made possible by earlier experiments with materials and construction, the most important of which led to the development of wrought iron and the commercial manufacture of flat glass.

The structural advantages of wrought iron over cast iron had been recognized from the earlier use of the 'hammered' version of wrought iron. (There is in fact no physical or chemical difference between the blacksmith's hammered form of wrought iron and industrially rolled wrought iron.) It had been known that wrought iron was less brittle, stronger in tension and structurally more reliable. However, the earlier hammered form of wrought iron demanded excessive labour to produce and, in consequence, was too expensive for general use. Henry Cort experimented with new methods of producing wrought iron and in 1783 took out a patent for the successful puddling process. This opened the way towards economic production and so, by the 1820s, wrought iron had become commercially available.

The cylinder method of making flat glass (in which a balloon of hot glass is swung to elongate it into a cylinder, which is then cut and laid out flat) was introduced into Britain in 1567 from Lorraine and Bohemia. Crown glass (in which hot glass is spun into a thick flat disc) was introduced into Britain from Normandy during the late seventeenth century. Plate glass (produced by pouring molten glass over a flat bed of sand and then, when it is cold, grinding and polishing it) was first produced in Britain at Ravenshead in 1773. Its use, however, was limited by high production costs.

Experiments using glass and wrought iron were carried out by the horticulturist J. S. Loudon. His interest was to improve the efficiency and appearance of horticultural hothouses, to make English hothouses look beautiful in their own right instead of being merely lean-to glazed sheds[4].

Loudon elected to use cylinder flat glass for his hothouses as it was lighter in weight than crown glass and thus reduced the load on the structure. This also reduced the amount of excise duty to be paid, which since 1746 had been calculated according to the weight of glass used. These experiments enabled him to produce a wrought-iron glazing bar which could be curved without reducing its strength; by 1816 he had produced a bar only 13 mm across.

In 1818, Loudon transferred the rights in his designs to the contractors Ward D. Bailey, enabling him to devote his time to writing, and in 1822 he published the first edition of his influential *An Encyclopaedia of Gardening* which contained details of his wrought-iron glazing bar and other constructional information.

One of the early hothouses built using Loudon's principles was in 1827 for Mrs Beaumont of Bretton Hall, Yorkshire (Figure 2.2). This was 30 metres in diameter and 18 metres high. It realized the

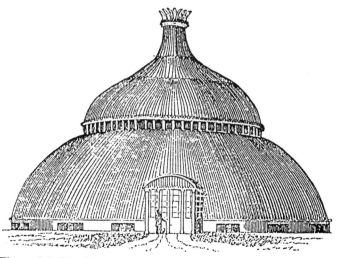

Figure 2.2 The Conservatory, Bretton Hall, Yorkshire, 1827; J. S. Loudon

horticulturist's ideal of maximum sunlight through a lightweight construction, and this uncompromised transparency made it one of the first curvilinear houses to break away from historical precedent[5]. It made no architectural reference to the orangeries and summer-houses which had been fashionable from the beginning of the eighteenth century. These, like the orangeries at Kensington Palace (1704) and at Kew Gardens (1761), took the form of a series of well-fenestrated classical pavilions. The hothouse at Bretton represented something new. It is regrettable that so little is recorded about this structure as it was taken down, after only five years, when Mrs Beaumont died in 1832. There is, however, a contemporary recollection of its construction written by Loudon[6]:

> There were no rafters or principal ribs for strengthening the roof besides the common wrought-iron sash-bar. . . . This caused some anxiety, for when the iron work was put up, before it was glazed, the slightest wind put the whole of it in motion. . . . as soon as the glass was put in, however, it was found to become perfectly firm and strong.

The conservatory at Syon House is interesting for its transitional position in history. Built in 1827 by Charles Fowler, its fine light metal and glass dome stands as an almost separate structure from the classical stone pavilions (Figure 2.3).

In 1819 the French government imposed a tax on the importation of iron with the purpose of stimulating their own iron industry. By the 1830s France had caught up with Britain in the technology of iron construction. They also were building large conservatories as the hothouse of the Jardin des Plantes, Paris, 1833–4, by Charles Rohault de Fleury[7]. The present structure, built in 1907 as a facsimile of the original, is a more straightforward rectilinear building than the English equivalent.

The manufacture of flat glass using the cylinder method was improved in 1832 by Robert Chance and George Bontemps. By producing larger balloons and laying them out on glass rather than sand, they were able to increase the size of the sheet to 250 mm by 900 mm (Figure 2.4). This economic glass was called broad or sheet glass.

The use of glass construction was further stimulated by Joseph Paxton through building the Great Stove at Chatsworth in 1836–40 (Figure 2.5). Paxton, then head gardener to the sixth Duke of Devonshire, was faced with the formidable task of building a large conservatory to house the newly imported exotic and large plants and trees. His experiments, pursued through several earlier conservatories

Figure 2.3 The Conservatory, Syon House, Isleworth, London, 1827; Charles Fowler (photograph James Strike)

at Chatsworth, led to the ridge and furrow form of glazing which overcame the problem of drainage by using what became known as the 'Paxton Gutter' (Figure 2.17). This form of construction enabled him, aided by the architect Decimus Burton, to build the Great Stove with a cross section 37.5 metres wide and 20.4 metres high (Figures 2.6 and 2.7). It was considered at the time to be without rival in Europe[8].

Queen Victoria visited the Great Stove at Chatsworth in 1843 and in the following year commissioned Decimus Burton to construct a similar glasshouse for the Royal Botanical Gardens at Kew (Figure 2.8). This building, the Palm House, erected during 1844–8, is

Figure 2.4 The cylinder method of making broad sheet glass, 1830s; Chance Brothers Ltd

Figure 2.5 The Great Stove, Chatsworth, Derbyshire, 1836–40; Joseph Paxton and Decimus Burton

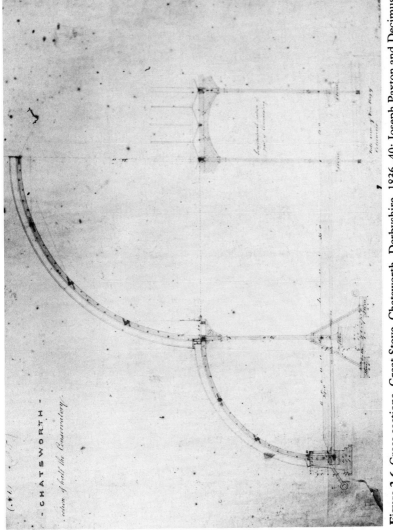

Figure 2.6 Cross sections, Great Stove, Chatsworth, Derbyshire, 1836–40; Joseph Paxton and Decimus Burton (courtesy of the Architectural Press photographic library)

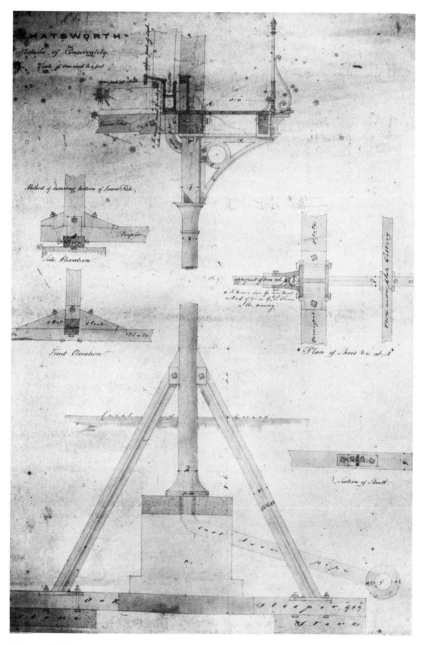

Figure 2.7 Construction details, Great Stove, Chatsworth, Derbyshire, 1836–40; Joseph Paxton and Decimus Burton (courtesy of the Architectural Press photographic library)

Figure 2.8 The Palm House, Kew Gardens, London, 1844–8; Decimus Burton and Richard Turner (photograph James Strike)

significant for its early use of structural wrought iron. Decimus Burton worked on the project with the Irish horticulturist Richard Turner, and it was Turner's earlier experience in working with Loudon's wrought-iron glazing bars which led to the use of structural wrought iron at Kew. During the erection of the building, Turner replaced the proposed cast-iron purlins and ribs with rolled I-section wrought-iron members similar to the 'deck-beams' which were being developed for use in shipbuilding by Kennedy and Vernon[9]. This resulted in a much lighter structure. Comparison of the new wrought-iron ribs with the cast-iron ribs originally specified in the contract drawings shows that the depth of the deck beams was halved, the width of the bulbous flange was also halved, and the width of the web was reduced to approximately one-fifth that of the cast rib. This reduction in the scale was accompanied by an even greater reduction in the weight, which allowed for a substitution of much smaller columns[10].

The Palm House is also interesting for its recognition of the high-tensile strength of wrought iron. The hollow cast-iron tubes between the ribs have wrought-iron tie-rods through them which,

Figure 2.9 Tie rods, Palm House, Kew Gardens, London, 1844–8; Decimus Burton and Richard Turner (photograph James Strike)

when tightened, form an effective system of knitting the whole structure together (Figure 2.9). Turner patented this idea in 1846[11].

The exploration of wrought iron in buildings was concurrent with, and also influenced by, the use of wrought iron in civil engineering projects. Of particular importance in this field was the work of Sir William Fairburn, who tested wrought iron and built the first large-scale wrought-iron structure, the Britannia Railway Bridge of 1845–50. Fairburn, with Turner, went on to build the 47.5 metres span structure for the station shed at Liverpool, Limestreet in 1846–51; this was the first shed to use iron throughout[12]. John Dobson improved the technique of rolling long wrought-iron curved sections and, with Robert Stephenson, built the first arched-roof station shed at Newcastle, 1848–50.

Also of importance was the work in tensile iron carried out in the 1840s by John Roebling in America. His practical experiments developed the pioneering work on iron ropes which had been started in Germany. His development, pursued against cynical opposition, led eventually to the building of the influential Brooklyn Suspension Bridge, 1867–83.

The new-found strength of wrought iron presented fresh potential to the designer. Large spans and vaults were now possible without the need to use large timber trusses or heavy brick vaults. Large free floor areas could now be spanned with lightweight construction resting on lightweight supporting walls.

Alongside this stimulus towards a new architectural language was another evolution in constructional technique. The notion of prefabrication, inherent in the manufacture of cast-iron objects, arose simultaneously with the construction of the first cast-iron buildings. The iron frames inside the mill buildings of the later eighteenth century were prefabricated, as were the churches built in Liverpool by Rickman and Cragg between 1812 and 1815.

The idea of prefabrication was also stimulated by the need to provide shelter for the early settlers in the outposts of the expanding British Empire. In the early 1830s, manufacturers in England were making small wooden houses, built in sections and packed especially for export to the Empire. A patent for the manufacture of corrugated iron was taken out by Richard Walker in 1837 and 'improved building kits', using this new waterproof cladding material and with cast-iron frame members, soon became popular (Figure 2.10). The visual

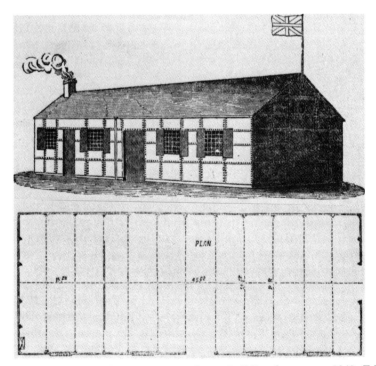

Figure 2.10 Prefabricated iron warehouse building for export, 1849; Edward T. Bellhouse and Co.

grammar of these sectional buildings had nothing to do with the landscape or indigenous materials of the South African Cape or the Swan River Valley in Australia; their appearance was the result of repetitious bolted sections, the lines of the corrugated iron, and a veneer of fashionable motifs moulded into the surface of the iron units.

Prefabrication was also used by James Bogardus in New York for the factory of 1848 at the corner of Centre and Ducine Streets (Figure 2.11) and the Laing Apartment Store of 1849 at the junction of Washington and Murray Street (Figure 2.12)[13]. The importance of these buildings lies in the resolute way in which Bogardus uses prefabrication, particularly the idea of the preformed cast-iron exterior panels bolted back to the iron frame. He was keen to publicize the economic and fireproof qualities of this early form of 'applied curtain wall', albeit the outward appearance was governed more by his use of cast historical motifs than by the system of construction. The drawing which he used to publicize his fireproof construction (Figure 2.13) anticipates the visual design freedom made possible by the steel frame.

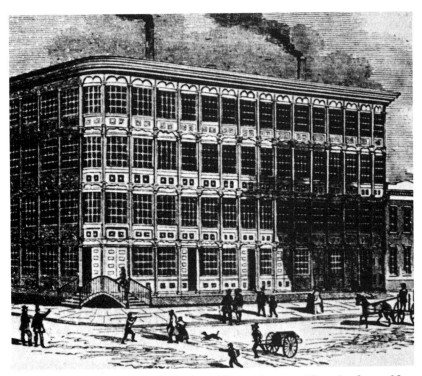

Figure 2.11 Cast iron factory, Junction of Centre Street and Duncine Street, New York, 1848; James Bogardus

Figure 2.12 Detail of the historical motifs on the cast-iron cladding panels, Laing Apartment Store, junction of Washington Street and Murray Street, New York, 1849; James Bogardus (reproduced from *Architectural Review*, February 1970, courtesy of Architectural Review)

Figure 2.13 Drawing to demonstrate the fire resistance of cast iron construction, 1856; James Bogardus

In London, Charles Barry with Pugin were also using precast iron parts for the Houses of Parliament, 1840–50. Of particular interest are the one metre square iron plates, riveted and caulked to form the roof covering.

All these developments, particularly in the use of iron, glass and prefabrication, were to come together in the building of the Crystal Palace in 1851 (Figure 2.14). The synthesis of these new forms of construction created the architectural language of the period.

The events leading up to the building of the Crystal Palace provide an interesting insight into the architectural attitudes of the time. HRH

Figure 2.14 (a) The Crystal Palace, Hyde Park, London, 1851; Joseph Paxton

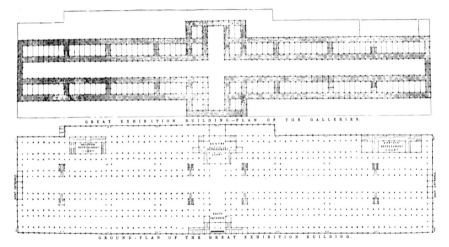

Figure 2.14 (b) Plan, Crystal Palace, Hyde Park, London, 1851; Joseph Paxton (courtesy of the Architectural Press photographic library)

Prince Albert wished to stage a Great Exhibition to stimulate international trade. Henry Cole administratively set this up and Joseph Paxton solved the building problem. It took time for Henry Cole to reach preliminary agreement with the manufacturers and the city concerning finance and to persuade both Parliament and public opinion that the proposed new building would not permanently scar Hyde Park. A Royal Commission was eventually set up in January 1850, leaving only sixteen months before the opening of the exhibition, planned for May 1851. In the following month the Commission set up an open competition for the design of a building to house the exhibition, and during the next three months they received 245 schemes. The Building Committee, set up by the Commission, rejected them all. It is regrettable that only two of the submissions have survived; these, by Hector Horeau and Richard Turner (Figures 2.15a and b), give an idea of the strange historicism that was fashionable at the time. The Building Committee included such eminent engineers and architects as Charles Barry, William Cubitt, C. R. Cockerell, Robert Stephenson and Isambard Brunel. In June 1850 they submitted and gained approval for an alternative scheme which they had themselves produced (Figure 2.15c). It was made public on 25 June. Brunel's engineering prowess was the principal contribution to the committee's scheme, a design which was described as a vast, squat, brick warehouse four times the length and twice the width of St Paul's Cathedral, adorned with a monstrous sheet-iron dome, which, even though it was bigger than that of the cathedral, would have looked like a bowler hat on a billiard table[14].

Opposition came from all quarters, and the full horror was confirmed in *The Times* on 27 June 1850:

> We are not to have a 'booth', nor a mere timber shed, but a solid, substantial edifice of brick and iron, and stone, calculated to endure the wear and tear of the next hundred years. In fact, a building is about to be erected in Hyde Park as substantial as Buckingham Palace. Can anyone be weak enough to suppose that a building erected on such a scale will ever be removed?

Not only was there outrage against the appearance and the permanence of the committee's design, but there also remained the question of it being built within the remaining ten months. It was estimated that it would require over sixteen million bricks. (This may be compared with the Euston Railway Terminus, built in 1835–9 by Philip and P. C. Hardwick, which used twenty million bricks in ten months; this was only possible owing to the extensive stocks available in the brickyards at that time.) The substantial edifice planned for Hyde Park would therefore take up most of the country's brickmaking capacity and other building works would have to stop for over a year. The Commission became progressively more uneasy about their design for the building.

A crisis existed and Joseph Paxton came forward with a solution. He had, through an introduction by Mr Ellis MP, held a private meeting with Cole on 11 June 1850 when he learned of the Commission's concern about the building. The specification for the contractor's tender was due to be sent out in only two weeks' time. Paxton realized that the problem could only be solved by using prefabricated units and

(a)

(b)

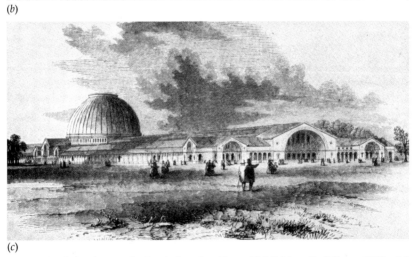

(c)

Figure 2.15 Designs submitted for the Great Exhibition Building, 1850: (a) Hector Horeau, (b) Richard Turner, (c) The Commissioners

a repetitive form of lightweight construction. He had two weeks in which to convince the Commission. He promised Cole that he would produce the principal working drawings within nine days, in spite of the important commitments which he had planned for the following few days. It was while presiding over a meeting of the Midland Railway Company's disciplinary meeting at Derby that he produced the famous 'blotting paper sketch' for the Crystal Palace (Figure 2.16). The principal drawings were produced in seven days with the help of Robert Barlow, an engineering draughtsman, who was able to advise

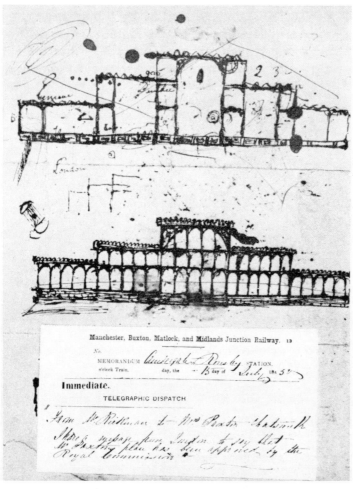

Figure 2.16 The 'Blotting Paper Sketch' for the Crystal Palace, 1850; Joseph Paxton (courtesy of the photographic library and the Board of Trustees of the Victoria and Albert Museum)

on the stresses in the structural members. The scheme was quickly approved and the contract let to Messrs Fox, Henderson and Company.

The design for the Crystal Palace was influenced by the speed with which it had to be built and the need for it to look lightweight and temporary in its setting at Hyde Park. It was built entirely from iron, wood and glass, made possible by the repeal of the tax on glass in 1851. It required a highly efficient organization and close co-operation between Paxton and the contractors. The working details were drawn up by Fox, and Henderson organized the production of the ironwork and other necessary materials. The components came from all over the country: the wrought-iron beams to span the central nave were produced by Fox and Henderson in their Birmingham works; the cast-iron columns and girders were sub-contracted to two firms at Dudley; wooden components were made in Chelsea; and the million square feet of glass were produced by the Birmingham firm of Chance Brothers[15]

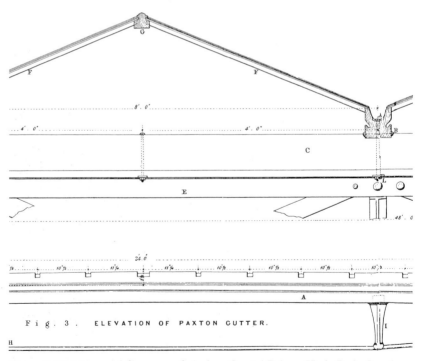

Fig. 3. ELEVATION OF PAXTON CUTTER.

Figure 2.17 Ridge and furrow roof glazing, Crystal Palace, Hyde Park, London, 1851; Joseph Paxton (reproduced from *The Building Erected in Hyde Park for the Great Exhibition*, Charles Downes)

The controlling dimension for the whole building came from the need to standardize the components for efficient prefabrication. The selected module of 8 feet came from the maximum spacing of the Paxton gutters in the ridge and furrow roof glazing. This was determined by the maximum length of 16 oz glass, which at that time was 49 inches (Figure 2.17). The 8 ft module generated the 24 ft structural bay used throughout the building, the 48 ft wide floor openings, and the 72 ft span (exploiting the full potential strength of wrought iron) over the nave and the vaulted central transept. Charles Downes, in his full survey *The Building Erected in Hyde Park for the Great Exhibition*, produced in 1852, refers to the impact of this standardization and prefabrication (Figure 2.18):

> It not only facilitates and economizes all of the operations by the frequent repetition of the same parts, but it also produces perfect symmetry in the building, and creates beautiful effects by the long vistas which are seen between the columns in every diagonal direction as well as in the longitudinal and transverse views.

The exterior diameter of the iron columns was kept constant by adjusting the internal diameter and thickness of metal according to the particular load carried by the column. The building consisted of a framework of visually identical columns and girders which were rigidly jointed to give lateral stiffness. Charles Downes wrote:

Figure 2.18 Interior, Crystal Palace, Hyde Park, London, 1851; Joseph Paxton

The columns and girders thus connected may be compared to an ordinary four-legged table in which the side rails, which support the upper surface, are firmly fixed to the legs.

It was only at the crossing of the central transept that the columns needed to be doubled up.

While the building was constructed using an industrialized structural system, opinion was not yet ready for an uncompromising design statement in such a prestigious public building. The stark simplicity of the structural solution was softened by the incorporation of 'historical stone' motifs in the ironwork. The transition from the circular columns to the faceted beam connections was made via an 'Early English' capital (Figure 2.19). The external bracing members were curved to give the elevation the appearance of an arched colonnade, and the skyline was adorned with 'Italian Gothic' crestings (Figure 2.20).

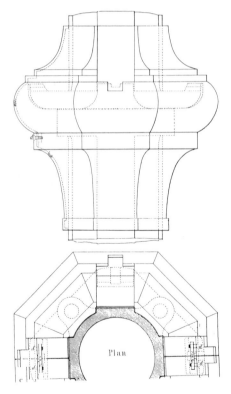

Figure 2.19 Capital of the columns, Crystal Palace, Hyde Park, London, 1851; Joseph Paxton (reproduced from *The Building Erected at Hyde Park for the Great Exhibition*, Charles Downes)

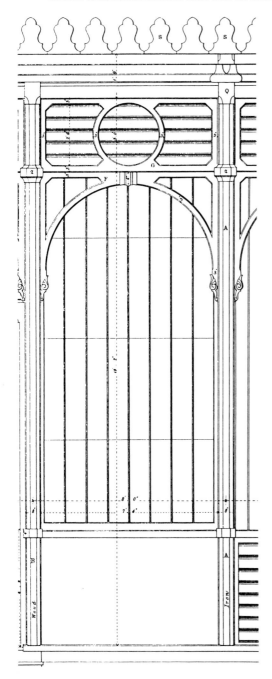

Figure 2.20 Exterior bay, Crystal Palace, Hyde Park, London, 1851; Joseph Paxton (reproduced from *The Building Erected at Hyde Park for the Great Exhibition*, Charles Downes)

This visual softening of the new form of construction can also be seen in the building of Paddington Station (1852–4), where Matthew Digby Wyatt was commissioned to add decorative Gothic tracery to Brunel's iron structure (Figure 2.21).

The respectability associated with historical stone buildings was very important to a large number of influential people in the 1850s. There was a great deal of debate, often acrimonious, about the effect of the new forms of construction on the design of buildings, especially public buildings where pomp and prestige were important. It must be noted that the new forms of construction had not affected domestic architecture at this time. Decimus Burton built himself a Gothic cottage at Tunbridge Wells[16] and Isambard Kingdom Brunel pursued a somewhat picturesque approach in his purchase and development of an estate at St Marychurch near Torquay in Devon[17].

The modernity of the Crystal Palace certainly divided the critics. Pugin, the Gothicist and ardent Catholic, hated it. He called it the 'Crystal Humbug' and the 'Glass Monster'. Ruskin called it 'a greenhouse larger than any greenhouse ever built before' and final proof that higher beauty was 'eternally impossible' in iron[18]. In 1853, in *The Seven Lamps of Architecture*, Ruskin wrote[19]:

Perhaps the most fruitful source of corruption which we have to guard against in recent times is . . . the use of iron. The art of architecture having been, up to

Figure 2.21 Decorated iron structure, Paddington Station, 1852–4; Brunel and Watt (photograph Edgar Jones)

the present century, practised for the most part in clay, stone, or wood, it has resulted that the sense of proportion and the laws of structure have been based on the employment of these materials; and that the employment of metallic framework would, therefore, be generally felt as a departure from the first principles of the art.

However, he went on to say:

Abstractly there appears no reason why iron should not be used as well as wood, and the time is probably near when a new system of architectural laws will be developed, adapted entirely to metallic construction.

This is interesting as it indicates that his objections were primarily aimed at the use of iron to emulate the pre-nineteenth century principles of construction.

Henry Cole set up the *Journal of Design* in 1849 in an attempt to lead inventors and manufacturers towards a better understanding of design. An edition of this journal in 1851 included an article by Mattthew Digby Wyatt to support and praise the Crystal Palace:

It has become difficult to decide where civil engineering ends and architecture begins. . . . From such beginnings, what glories may be in reserve, when England has systematized a scale of form and proportion. . . . we may trust ourselves to dream. . . . it is impossible to disregard the fact that the building for the Exhibition is likely to accelerate the consummation devoutly to be wished and that the novelty of its form and details will be likely to exercise a powerful influence upon national taste.

Gottfried Semper visited the Crystal Palace Exhibition, and in 1852 wrote his essay *Wissenschaft, Industrie und Kunst* (Science, Industry and Art) in which he examined the impact of industrialization and mass consumption on the entire field of applied art and architecture:

Unremittingly science enriches itself and life with newly discovered useful materials, . . . new methods and techniques, with new tools and machines . . .

and in response to conservative attitudes about materials and construction:

The hardest porphyry and granite are cut like butter and polished like wax, ivory is softened and pressed into shapes, caoutchouc and gutta percha are vulcanized and used to produce deceptive imitations of carvings in wood, metal or stone.

There can be no doubt that the Crystal Palace brought to a head the debate about the effect that industrialization and the use of iron and glass in construction were to have on architectural attitudes and design.

3 Pioneers of concrete construction 1820–1900

During the first half of the nineteenth century a series of experiments took place which helped to develop concrete into a new and exciting building material.

Although various forms of naturally occurring cementicious materials had been used even earlier than the Roman period, it is in the construction of the large Roman baths and amphitheatres that the advantages of concrete construction can first be recognized. The Romans made use of the cementicious quality of crushed pozzolana as a binding agent, and they also experimented with strips of bronze as reinforcement; this failed, however, owing to the differential rates of expansion of the pozzolana concrete and the bronze reinforcement[1].

The regular use of cements in Britain began in the 1770s with the introduction of stucco work[2]. Experiments were carried out to find a suitable binding agent and numerous rival mixtures were marketed. Many of these failed but a few became successful, notably the Reverend John Liardet's Patented Cement of 1773, which had a linseed oil base and which was bought out by the Adam Brothers in 1774 and became known as Adam's Cement[3]; the Reverend James Parker's Patented Cement of 1796, an early form of hydraulic cement which later became known as Roman Cement[4]; and Dihl's Mastic of 1815 which was based on linseed oil with litharge and china clay[5].

However, in relation to concrete as it is known today, the story opens in 1794 when Joseph Aspdin carried out early experiments to produce an artificial cement by heating chalk and clay together[6]. In 1811 a patent was taken out by James Frost based on similar experiments, and in 1824 Aspdin took out the important Portland Cement Patent. It is interesting to note his choice of the descriptive word 'Portland' as it implies 'artificial stone'; it is likely that he saw his cement more as an external grade of rendering to produce, relatively cheaply, the appearance of blocks of Portland Stone[7]. At this time

Portland cement was considered not as a new material with its own characteristics and architectural language, but, like the other stuccos, as an artificial substitute for expensive natural stone.

This patent was followed by a period of experimentation in Britain, France and the USA. In an atmosphere of rivalry and acrimonious polemic numerous patents were taken out, some of them based on indistinguishable originality. It is difficult to isolate distinctive examples, but the following each represent a significant architectural statement.

The first concrete house was built in 1835 for John White at Swanscombe, Kent (Figure 3.1). It had concrete walls, concrete roof tiles, concrete window frames and concrete decorative features. It was designed to look like any other Victorian house but used concrete as a substitute for conventional materials.

From 1850, the French contractor François Coignet developed a technique of strengthening an iron skeleton framework by encasing it in concrete. The earliest example was a concrete villa built in 1853 at 72 Rue Charles-Michels, St Denis (Figure 3.2). This villa, by the architect Théodore Lachèz, again used concrete to imitate the moulded elevations of the classical design. In 1864 Coignet constructed

Figure 3.1 Concrete house for John White, Swanscombe, Kent, 1835 (courtesy of the British Cement Association photographic library)

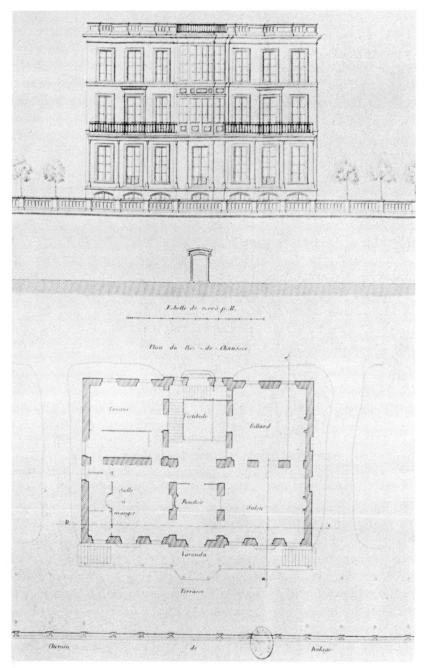

Figure 3.2 72 Rue Charles-Michels, St Denis, 1853; François Coignet and Théodore Lachèz (reproduced from *Concrete, A Vision of the New Architecture*, Peter Collins, courtesy of Faber and Faber, first published in *L'Ingénieur*, 1 November 1855)

Figure 3.3 Concrete church, Le Vésinet, 1864; François Coignet and L. C. Boileau (reproduced from *Concrete, A Vision of the New Architecture*, Peter Collins, courtesy of Faber and Faber, first published in *Builder*, 11 November 1865)

the concrete church at Le Vésinet designed in the Gothic Revival style by L. C. Boileau (Figure 3.3).

The fireproof quality of concrete was exploited for the floors of cotton and woollen mills. The wine and spirit store erected in Bridge Street, Reading, in about 1870 (Figure 3.4) was one of the largest concrete structures in Britain at the time[8]. It anticipated Owen Williams's concrete structures of the 1930s.

Research carried out by Christopher Stanley of the Cement and Concrete Association confirms that the origins of reinforced concrete, in terms of an understanding of the structural interaction between the

Figure 3.4 Wine and spirits store, Bridge Street, Reading, Berkshire, *c*.1870 (courtesy of the British Cement Association photographic library)

iron and the concrete, should be attributed to William Wilkinson. Stanley writes[9]:

> . . . the man who is generally credited with the invention of reinforced concrete is a little-known Newcastle builder, William Wilkinson. His biggest claim to fame is his patent, first applied for in 1854, for 'Improvement in the construction of fireproof dwellings, warehouses, and other buildings'.

In this patent Wilkinson describes the layout of reinforcement in the concrete and identifies the iron, set in a low position, acting in tension.

Successful experiments were carried out in France by Joseph Monier during the 1860s. He took out several important patents but, in the 1880s, sold these rights to the German engineering company Wayss and Freytag. Details of Monier's methods were published by G. A. Wayss in 1887 in *Morrierbau*.

It was, however, François Hennebique who developed reinforced concrete into a cogent system of construction. Hennebique, a builder in France, saw the potential of reinforced concrete and pursued

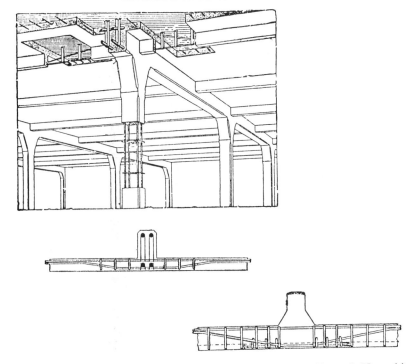

Figure 3.5 Patent for monolithic reinforced concrete, 1892; François Hennebique (reproduced from *Hennebique Ferro-concrete Catalogue, 4th edition, 1921*, courtesy of John Fiddler library)

extensive experiments which led to his patent in 1892. The patent shows his method of jointing to achieve a monolithic type of reinforced concrete (Figure 3.5).

Hennebique used this form of construction in 1895 for the Charles VI Spinning Mill at Tourcoing (Figure 3.6); here the system of concrete construction began to influence the appearance of the building. He built several other projects and his company became associated with a standardized form of detailing structural concrete. In 1897 his partner L. G. Mouchel set up a firm of civil engineers in London specializing in the use of Mouchel–Hennebique Ferro-Concrete. The first building to be constructed using their system was the Weaver and Company Provender Mill (Figure 3.7)[10].

The Weaver Mill, built in 1897–8 at the North Dock, Swansea, represents an important landmark in the evolution of reinforced concrete construction. It was the first concrete building to demonstrate the design characteristics inherent in the use of reinforced concrete.

Figure 3.6 Charles Six Spinning Mill, Tourcoing, Lille, 1895; François Hennebique (reproduced from *Concrete, A Vision of the New Architecture*, Peter Collins, credited to Charles Six Spinning Mill)

The structural system was expressed and the concrete left exposed. The surface of the concrete was lightly brushed after striking the shutter to achieve an exposed aggregate finish (except for the cornice, which was rendered)[11]. Most significant, however, was the 4.25 metre projection of the curved structural cantilever over the loading bay at the end of the building. This prominent feature, which took the 670 tonne total weight of the end bay, was a seminal expression of the tensile stresses in reinforced concrete. Its shape demonstrated an understanding of the forces acting within the structure. Henry C. Portsmouth, architect for the project, obviously had respect for the Hennebique system of construction, and let the system dictate the appearance of the building with the structure standing unembellished[12].

Plans to demolish the building in the mid 1970s caused a dispute between the local authority and the Welsh Office. *The Western Mail* of 25 February 1976 reported hundreds of letters from the public and leading preservation groups recommending that it should be saved.

Figure 3.7 Weaver and Company Provender Mill, North Dock, Swansea, 1897–8; François Hennebique and Henry Portsmouth (reproduced from *Hennebique Ferro-concrete Catalogue, 4th edition, 1921*, courtesy of John Fiddler library)

Questions were raised in the House of Commons and the Secretary of State agreed that the Weaver Mill should be a Listed Building. Regrettably the building was demolished in 1984.

In America, confidence in the structural use of reinforced concrete led to the building in 1902 of the 16-storey Ingall's Building, Cincinnati (Figure 3.8). It was constructed by the Ferro-Concrete Construction Company and the engineer for the company was E. L. Ransome. The building, designed by the architects Elzner and Anderson, extended the proven structural capabilities of reinforced concrete but did little to clarify the design language of this form of construction.

As the use of concrete increased during the nineteenth century, so debate about its suitability became more heated. In England the subject stimulated much interest and was discussed at length by the Architectural Association in 1868 and 1871, and again by The Royal

Figure 3.8 Ingall's Building, Cincinnati, 1902; E. L. Ransome with Elzner and Anderson (reproduced from *Concrete, A Vision of the New Architecture*, Peter Collins, credited to Prof. G. L. Martin and Russell Potter)

Institute of British Architects in 1871 and 1876. Much of the discussion was caused by the dissatisfaction which most people felt for the drab and inconsistent colour and the uneven surface of concrete. However, S. Cockerell considered the 'honeycomb' appearance of concrete to be quite natural, and others defended this honesty. *The Builder* of 24 June 1871 refers to a few landlords who, like Mr Whatman MP of Maidstone, were content to forego a coating of stucco on their concrete cottages.

The early debate was primarily about the surface and texture of the new material, and it was not until the turn of the century that the general discussion turned towards the influence which the new shapes, inherent in reinforced concrete, were to have on architectural design.

4 Growth of the functional tradition 1855–1914

This chapter examines the architecture which developed, during the second half of the nineteenth century, out of the materials and techniques which emerged from the Industrial Revolution. It explores how these new methods of construction created a new architectural language.

One of the key factors was the straightforward and economic way in which the new materials and types of construction were used. This rational, honest and truthful outlook was prevalent, especially amongst industrialists, in Victorian England. Nikolaus Pevsner has written about English distrust of the extreme and about detachment, moderation and reasonableness[1]. The socialism of William Morris, Lethaby's devotion to education, and Ruskin's writing about the honesty of materials, all reflect an underlying need for truth. In speculation about the nature of a new architecture or a material, the problem tended to be seen as primarily ethical[2].

Functional construction was used in 1856 for a new building for the Museum of Practical Art, the institution which eventually became part of the Victoria and Albert Museum. The building (Figure 4.1) was a plain iron-framed structure over 80 metres long covered by sheets of corrugated iron. It was through the encouragement of Prince Albert that the new accommodation was provided. A previous scheme designed by Gottfried Semper having proved to be financially impractical, Prince Albert devised the idea of the pragmatic solutions to house the department until a new building could be built for the whole museum[3]. What is interesting to observe is that Prince Albert was prepared to allow such a rational building, lacking any of the historical references which would, at that time, be expected of an important building on an important site.

The building was constructed by Charles Younge and Company who specialized in supplying iron houses, hospitals, barracks, and other

(a)

(b)

Figure 4.1 (a) The 'Brompton Boilers', Museum of Practical Art (now The Victoria and Albert Museum), Kensington, London, 1856; Charles Younge and Company; (b) constructing the iron frame (countesy of the photographic library and the Board of Trustees of the Victoria and Albert Museum)

buildings to the British Colonies and America[4]. It soon became known as the 'Brompton Boilers', and *The Builder*, the leading architectural journal of the day, complained that our rulers at times found strange ways of demonstrating the value they attached to art in industry, and regretted that no professional architect had been consulted about the Museum building[5]. The commissioners, however, liked it and in a letter to the Chancellor of the Exchequer, applying for funds to build it, drew attention to its merits[6]:

> Irrespective of its simplicity and cheapness, and the remarkable facility with which it can be constructed, it enjoys the great advantage from a pecuniary point of view, of being designed of a material which possesses a permanent pecuniary value, to which the cost of the labour employed in its construction bears only a small proportion.

It was in this new institution that Captain Francis Fowke set up the Museum of Construction and Building Materials, which did much to promote new materials and techniques from both Britain and abroad.

The 'Brompton Boilers' building was ahead of its time; when, in the late 1860s, the structure was taken down and re-assembled to form the Bethnal Green Museum, it was clad, not with corrugated iron, but with a veneer of classical brickwork.

Another of the early buildings to use the modern methods of construction, and also achieve a complete break from the past, was the boatstore at Sheerness Dockyard (Figure 4.2). Designed by the Director of Engineering and Architectural Works at the Admiralty, Colonel Godfrey T. Greene, it was built in 1858–60. The boatstore is a four-storey building 64 metres long by 41 metres wide. It is divided in plan into bays 4.6 metres wide by 9.1 metres deep, each formed with H-section cast-iron columns and composite section wrought-iron main beams (Figure 4.3). Bracing against wind loading and other horizontal forces is achieved by rigid connections between the columns and beams. The elevation uses galvanized corrugated iron sheets and timber windows to infill between the exposed iron members of the structural frame. The functional approach is also seen in the rational and unconcealed internal fixings.

Several important points need to be noted about the construction. Firstly, Colonel Greene selected the contractors, Messrs Fox, Henderson and Company, who, having built the Crystal Palace, had considerable experience in the fabrication and assembly of iron members. Secondly, the beams were made up from simple wrought-iron sections riveted together, as these were all that the available rolling machinery could handle. Bars, angles and tees were

Figure 4.2 Boatstore, Sheerness Dockyard, Kent, 1858–60; Colonel Godfrey T. Greene (courtesy of the Architectural Press photographic library)

Figure 4.3 Junction of the column and beam, Boatstore, Sheerness Dockyard, Kent, 1858–60; Colonel Godfrey T. Greene (courtesy of the Architectural Press photographic library)

formed by passing wrought-iron billets through rollers. The beams were then built up from lengths of plate riveted with angles and tees. Wrought-iron sections were never standardized, being decided by a particular ironworks[7].

Thirdly, the construction represents a clear and recognizable step forward in the development of the iron frame. In earlier mill and warehouse buildings, the iron structure was contained within, restrained and partially supported by, an external loadbearing wall; at Sheerness, the skeleton frame becomes a four-storey complete and self-supporting structure. The French writer Abbé Laugier identified as early as the 1750s the significance of the structural frame. He advocated simple unadorned structures of posts, beams and a roof because 'that was how man built before architecture became contaminated with the notion of style'[8]. One can imagine that these ideas had both an intellectual and practical appeal to the early mill builders. At Sheerness, with the skeleton frame forming the structure for the entire building, the external enclosing wall is free to be formed in any non-loadbearing construction such as lightweight panels of corrugated iron sheets and long rows of windows.

Finally, the construction of the boatstore at Sheerness is both physically and visually direct and simple. It is explicit and uncompromised by style or historical precedent. The rational expression of the structural frame and the straightforward and unstylized formation of the non-loadbearing infill panels give the building a sense of fitness for purpose, a sense of functional construction. No doubt the strict adherence of the dockyard buildings to a functional approach had its roots in the anonymous idiom of the shipwright and the marine engineer, who introduced into this architecture that combination of toughness, neatness and economy encountered in everything connected with the sea[9].

This functional toughness is seen in the construction of the ironclad naval gunships which were being introduced at this time. HMS *Warrior*, launched in 1860[10], was clad with large wrought-iron plates each weighing four tonnes (Figure 4.4)[11]. The plates, 4.5 × 1 metre and 115 mm thick, demonstrate not only the capability of the heavy iron industry but also the sophistication of the tongue-and-groove edge joints and countersunk-bolt fixings of this early form of metal cladding.

The advent of the structural iron frame had a considerable effect on the external appearance of buildings, particularly noticeable as an increase in window area. This tendency began in the early mills in

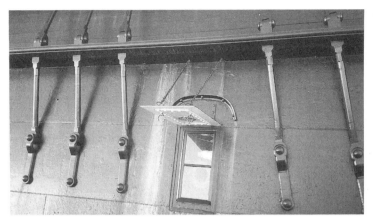

Figure 4.4 Iron cladding, HMS Warrior, Portsmouth, Hampshire, 1860 (photograph James Strike)

Figure 4.5 Stanley Mill, Stonehouse, 1813 (courtesy of the Architectural Press photographic library)

response to the practical need to provide more light in buildings with a deeper floor plan, and also as a result of general improvement in philanthropic attitudes. Compare Ditherington Mill of 1796, with a 6% window area (Figure 1.12), and Stanley Mill at Stonehouse of 1813, with a 40% window area (Figure 4.5). It was only when the iron frame eliminated the need for the external fabric to be loadbearing that the potential of large window areas could be fully achieved.

The concept of expressed frame with glazed infill panels can be traced through a series of buildings. It is recognizable in the Harper Bros Store, New York, built by James Bogardus in 1854, and in several influential buildings erected in Glasgow between 1855 and 1860. Gardner's Store, 36 Jamaica Street, Glasgow (Figure 4.6) was built in 1855–6 by John Baird; it is graceful in appearance, straightforward and logical in its use of materials. Although it is laden with classical references, the grid of the structural frame is apparent and the infill within the frame is predominantly glazed to give the building an extraordinary sense of lightness[12]. A contemporary

Figure 4.6 Gardner's Store, Jamaica Street, Glasgow, 1855–6; John Baird (photograph James Strike)

account of Gardner's Store in the *Illustrated London News* of March 1856 describes the modern impression which the building gave:

> This edifice . . . of striking character, whether as regards novelty of design or materials. . . . The two fronts are composed entirely of cast-iron and British plate glass. . . . The general features of the building are . . . lightness of construction, giving great admission of light, unobstructed floor room, and facility of division, to suit different classes of tenants.

This account brings out three important design issues. Firstly, the tax on glass having been abolished in 1851, by 1855 the use of large heavy sheets of plate glass had become feasible. This had the considerable

Figure 4.7 Rear elevation, Northern Insurance Building, 84–94 St Vincent Street, Glasgow, 1908–9; John A. Campbell

effect of enlarging the visual grain and scale of buildings. Secondly, the use of the iron frame provided a new type of open floor plan, interrupted only by the grid of columns. Thirdly, this type of floor plan encouraged a flexible arrangement of non-loadbearing internal partitions. While the public facades of Gardner's Store still use historical references, albeit subdued, the interior construction is of the direct and unstylized type used at Sheerness.

This approach is also seen in other buildings constructed in Glasgow at the turn of the century; for example, the side elevation of Lion Chambers of 1905–6[13], designed by James Salmon with J. Gaff Gillespie, and the rear elevation of the Northern Insurance building of 1908–9 (Figure 4.7), by John A. Campbell. However, functional construction is used only at the rear of these properties; the public facades retain strong links with traditional Scottish design.

The Uniroyal factory, Dumfries, of 1909–12 (Figure 4.8)[14], probably designed and constructed by Trussed Concrete Steel Co Ltd, uses a concrete frame to form the elevation. Again the frame is infilled with large areas of glazing and the construction is straightforward and rational.

Figure 4.8 Uniroyal factory, Dumfries, Scotland, 1909–12 (courtesy of Dinardo and Partners)

A common factor in the type of functional construction used in Britain at the beginning of the twentieth century is that it was not at the time considered to be an important aspect of architectural design. Uniroyal factory had no architect, and Campbell's glazed facade looked onto the service yard. The potential of a design approach derived from the new materials and techniques was not recognized in Britain, but was taken up in Germany to become a significant contribution to what became known as the Modern Movement.

5 Development of the steel frame 1870–1914

One of the most important developments which influenced the evolution of building materials and building technique prior to World War I was the growth of steel production and the resultant evolution of steel-frame construction.

Steel had been produced as early as the 1740s using Benjamin Hunstan's uneconomic crucible process, the cementation process was introduced in 1772, and Henry Cort's puddling process in 1783. In the mid 1850s Henry Bessemer in England, and William Kelly in America, separately designed a converter for reducing the amount of carbon in iron to produce steel; this system was improved in 1867 by the open hearth process, developed in Birmingham by Siemens and Martin. By 1870 steel manufacture had become established and sufficiently economic to affect the building industry. The production of 'mild steel' (i.e. a low-carbon steel that is strong and malleable but not readily hardened or temperred) overtook that of wrought iron during the mid 1880s.

Steel was not subject to quality control and national standards as it is today. Information on strength was given by each manufacturer, and these figures were used to compile published textbooks. One of the most widely used of these was 'Twelvetrees' which, in 1900, tabulated the following values[1]:

	Tons/in^2 (as quoted)	N/mm^2 (approx. equivalent)
Cast iron (average values)		
Tensile strength	8	(120)
Compressive strength	38–50	(590–780)
Wrought iron		
Tensile strength	18–24	(280–370)
Compressive strength	16–20	(245–310)

	Tons/in^2 (as quoted)	N/mm^2 (approx. equivalent)
Mild steel		
Tensile strength	26–32	(400–495)

Of particular importance was the improvement in tensile strength, from cast iron of the 1790s at $120\,$N/mm^2 and wrought iron of the 1820s at $300\,$N/mm^2, up to mild steel of the 1870s at 400–495 N/mm^2. This allowed a change in the span:depth ratio of beams, the possibility of longer spans, and the possibility of carrying heavier loads. This contributed, in architectural terms, to the development of the structural steel frame.

It was in Europe that cast iron had been invented and developed as a building material and wrought iron had first influenced architecture. However, the potential of steel was first realized in the USA, where there was a large and buoyant construction market. By contrast, the restrictive approach in Britain is illustrated by the government's attitude to the problem of rust. In 1859, the engineer John Hawkshaw proposed to use structural steel for the Charing Cross railway bridge in London, but was refused permission by the Board of Trade which, for the next 20 years, would not allow steel to be used for any structural projects[2].

The surge of building and civil engineering projects in the USA during the second half of the nineteenth century enabled companies to invest the large sums of money needed to set up steel rolling mills. These mills produced great quantities of standard sections which were tabulated with their strengths in company handbooks. An early example was *The Phoenix Company Handbook* of 1869. The most influential, however, was the *Carnegie Pocket Companion* of 1873, which became recognized throughout the world[3].

The influence of steel on design may be traced through a series of structures built in the USA between 1870 and 1900. In architectural terms, this centred primarily around the skyscraper, a building type that grew from the spirit of competition and the desire to build structures as symbols of wealth, prestige and the vigour of the New World. The steel frame stimulated the urge to build higher and gave form to the towers. There was far less prejudice against change, less pressure to use historical precedents to govern the appearance of buildings.

The steel framed skyscraper began in Chicago. The disastrous fire in 1871, which destroyed virtually the whole of the centre of the city,

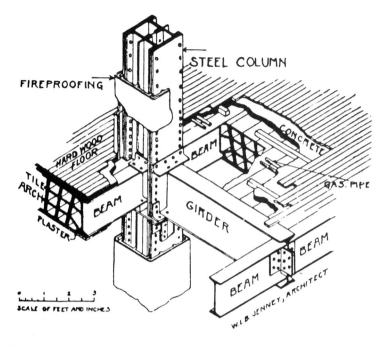

Figure 5.1 Fireproof steel frame construction, 1890; William Le Baron Jenney (reproduced from *Modern Architecture, a Critical History*, Kenneth Frampton)

provided an opportunity to start again, a need to build quickly and a need for fireproof construction. Many of the new buildings used fireproofed steel frames internally to support the floors (Figure 5.1), but it was not until 1885 that the first completely steel framed building was erected. This was the Home Insurance Building (Figure 5.2) designed by William Le Baron Jenney. It rose to twelve storeys and demonstrates, in spite of the veneer of classical detailing, the box shape and structural grid of the steel skeleton frame.

The architect Louis Sullivan made a considerable contribution to the development of the skyscraper. In his assay *The Tall Office Building Artistically Considered*, he recognized that a new form of architectural expression would come out of the new technology, that these new buildings would express a spirit of height, and that this expression would be without historical reference. This emphasis on verticality is the essence of the Wainwright Building, St Louis, 1891,

Figure 5.2 Home Insurance Building, Chicago, 1884–5; William Le Baron Jenney (reproduced from *History of the Skyscraper*, Francisco Mujica, courtesy of the British Architectural Library, RIBA, London)

Figure 5.3 Wainwright Building, St Louis, 1891; Alder and Sullivan (courtesy of the British Architectural Library, RIBA, London)

designed by Adler and Sullivan (Figure 5.3). It expresses Sullivan's aspiration[4] that the skyscraper:

> . . . must be tall, every inch of it tall. The force and power of altitude must be in it, the glory and pride of exultation must be in it. In must be every inch a proud and soaring thing, rising in sheer exaltation that from bottom to top it is a unit without a single dissenting line.

Towards the end of the nineteenth century, there still existed rivalry between the skeleton steel frame structure and the load-bearing masonry structure. The last of the solid masonry skyscrapers was the 16-storey Monadnock Building in Chicago by Burnham and Root,

Figure 5.4 Monadnock Building, Chicago, 1891; Burnham and Root (photograph John Adams)

1891 (Figure 5.4). This is a heavyweight of inert, thick walls punctured with holes for the windows. Compare this with the 15-storey skeleton frame Reliance Building of 1894 in Chicago by Burnham and Company (Figure 5.5). Here the steel frame allows the enclosing walls to become a lightweight open lattice of glass and tera cotta.

Even the American spirit of adventure for pushing the steel frame higher was temporarily held back by conservative opinion. The Chicago World Fair of 1893 was set up to show how America was leading the world, but in reality it turned into a collection of sham, white, neo-classical exhibition buildings full of old-fashioned articles. American taste was dragged down to such a level that what people considered to be an advance was actually a serious retrogression. This fashion during the period 1860 to 1890 led to the tag 'The Brown Decades' [5].

Traditional attitudes also led to the introduction of legislation to preserve the conventional view of daylight around buildings. This was

Figure 5.5 Reliance Building, Chicago, 1894; Burnham and Company (photograph John Adams)

introduced in Chicago in 1893 and immediately restricted the height of new buildings. Other cities imposed their own rules and, as a result of this legislation, the development of skyscraper building advanced only as restrictions were, over the decades, gradually relaxed.

In spite of these conservative attitudes, the inevitability of the steel frame was soon established in architecture. This is clearly seen in the Carson Pirie Scott Store of 1901–4 (Figure 5.6). This department store, originally constructed for Schlesinger and Mayer, was the last of the buildings designed by Louis Sullivan and illustrates his recognition of the relationship between the steel frame and architectural design. The elevations are formed from the cellular grid of the constructional steel frame and, in spite of the much-debated decorative handling of the ground floor, prefigure the gridded skyscrapers which were to follow.

Figure 5.6 Carson Pirie Scott Department Store, Chicago, 1901–4; Louis Sullivan (photograph Bastiaan Valkenburg)

The 19-storey Republic Building, Chicago, by Holabird and Roche, built in 1905–9 (Figure 5.7), gives a clear expression of what came to be known as the Chicago Frame style. There was plenty of confidence and competition, and by 1914 the steel frame had reached 42 storeys for the L. C. Smith building in Seattle.

Figure 5.7 Republic Building, Chicago, 1905–9; Holabird and Roche (reproduced from *Building to the Skies*, Alfred Bossom)

Figure 5.8 All-weather working on the skyscraper, 1914 (reproduced from *Building to the Skies*, Alfred Bossom)

The human drive and determination required in the erection of the early steel frames was enormous and illustrates the sense of energy and determination in the USA at the beginning of the twentieth century. Alfred Bossom, the English MP and architect who contributed to the building of many of the early American skyscrapers, clarifies this in *Building to the Skies* [6]:

> Skyscraper building is not child's play. It is an exceedingly hazardous calling. The toll it levies on nerve, physical strength and constitutional stamina is incessant. Among the steel erectors, whose Blondin-like feats fascinate the crowds in the streets below, few go for five years without a serious accident. . . . These men had an extraordinary dexterity in throwing hot rivets from the forge to the catcher's barrel twenty or thirty or forty feet away.

Bossom continues by describing how American workmen were provided with mackintoshes, long rubber boots and sou'westers. Tarpaulins were erected and a dozen fire braziers lit to overcome the problem of rain, snow, wind and freezing temperatures (Figure 5.8). The programme schedule was crucial in the USA and played an important part in the making of decisions about construction [7].

The examination of working practices became significant. Frederick Taylor, the American production engineer, developed principles of scientific management between 1895 and 1915. Managers used time charts and stop-watches to determine 'the one best way' of completing a project. Employees would then specialize in a specific, limited and simple task with the result that production increased to the benefit of all. Flat-top metal desks, mechanical conveyors and the production line symbolized the change, with materials such as steel signifying efficiency and economy [8].

The first large steel framed building in Britain was not built until 1906. This was The Ritz, Piccadilly, London, in 1906–7 by Arthur Davis with the French architect Charles Mewes. However, in its Beaux-Arts dressing it expressed nothing of the spirit of the steel frame.

6 Roots of the Modern Movement 1820–1914

Chapter 4 considered how the materials and building techniques which emerged in Britain during the second half of the nineteenth century led to rational forms of construction, and how this approach contributed to what became known as the Functional Tradition. We now continue the story by looking at the connections between this development and the origins of the Modern Movement in central Europe at the beginning of the twentieth century.

Both the Functional Tradition and the Modern Movement made use of modern building materials and modern constructional techniques. What then was the difference between them? Chapter 4 established that the criteria of the British Functional Tradition were to be found in the honest, reasonable and detached way in which the new materials and techniques were used. There was in Britain a reticence, a distrust of the extreme, and a lack of interest in the architectural outcome. In central Europe a different attitude developed: both the constructional process and the visual effect became the focus of the designer's thoughts. This awareness formed the catalyst for the Modern Movement.

It is necessary to consider what made the Modern Movement distinctive and what part construction played in that distinctiveness. The following two extracts form a useful starting point. First, Alison and Peter Smithson in *The Heroic Period of Modern Architecture* seek to define the new way of thinking at the beginning of the twentieth century[1]:

> What we are looking for is a building which is so different from those which preceded it as to establish a new architecture as a fact, not as a possibility.

Second, an extract from Dennis Sharp's *A Visual History of Twentieth Century Architecture*[2]:

> The generally accepted view by architectural historians that the introduction of

new materials almost miraculously caused a breakthrough on every sector of the design front is a myth. Virtually all the materials used, and most of the technical developments, had been tried years before in the previous century.

These extracts appear to question the hypothesis of this book; the Smithsons imply that the early buildings of the Modern Movement were completely new and had no ancestors, and Dennis Sharp implies that technical developments themselves did not produce the buildings of the Modern Movement. However, it is necessary to read the extracts within a broader context. The newness of the early buildings of the Modern Movement lay in the attitude to construction rather than in the actual materials or methods of assembly. The designers of the early buildings certainly took hold of nineteenth-century innovations in construction. Dennis Sharp captures the mood of that period in his introduction to the same book[2]:

> The nineteenth century was an age of rapid growth and unprecedented expansion in virtually every field of human endeavour, in which new ideas shot from the heads of inventors, industrialists, philosophers and artists like sparks from an early electric generator . . . forces excited by one fashionable current had an effect on others.

The early buildings of the Modern Movement came out of a process of synthesis which used 'electric sparks' not only from construction, but also from other important issues such as the Arts and Crafts Movement, the machine aesthetic and ideas of social concern; the various forces each had a stimulating effect on the others.

We need now to consider why the Modern Movement first flowered in central Europe. The initiative of industrial growth and adventure had, by the turn of the century, moved from Britain to be shared by America and central Europe. John Masefield captures the international scene in his contemporary poem *Cargoes* with its famous opening line 'Quinquireme of Nineveh from distant Ophir'. The closing verse describes Britain in a somewhat derisive tone:

> Dirty British Coaster with a salt-caked smoke stack
> Butting through the channel in the mad March days,
> With a cargo of Tyne coal,
> Road-rail, pig-lead,
> Firewood, iron-ware, and cheap tin trays.

Germany in particular was increasing its share of the new international markets, was training far more engineering students than Britain and, like America, had a less diffident temperament than Britain. Germany was therefore more receptive to the visual and cultural shock that was to accompany the Modern Movement.

This acceptance of change in the use of new materials and forms of construction led, in America, to the surge of steel towers and skyscrapers, and in France to the innovative concrete structures of Auguste Perret and Tony Garnier. It was, however, in central Europe that the spirit of the new materials and techniques was most consciously synthesized and recognized as a generator of architectural design.

Throughout the nineteenth century, connections had been made betwen Germany and Britain. Ideas and attitudes had been transferred through visits to Britain of several influential people, who were able to recognize the best ideas from British industry and building construction without becoming involved in the debate about historicism.

Reference was made in Chapter 1 to the visit to Britain in 1823 by B. C. W. von Beuth, the Prussian Minister of Commerce, and his further visit, with the architect Karl Friedrich Schinkel, in 1826. Beuth had been interested in the constructional systems used in the early mill buildings such as Ditherington and the Manchester Cotton Mills. He must have taken these impressions back with him to Germany where his influential position enabled him to spread his new-found interest and knowledge. No doubt it was through Beuth's influence that the Prussian Crown sponsored him, with Schinkel, to develop the investigation with their visit to Britain in 1826. Beuth was instructed to use his skills as an engineer to study the industrial developments which were having such a positive effect on the British economy. His return home with this information must have contributed to the new interest in the aesthetic of 'the industrial machine' which was germinating in Germany at that time. Schinkel's visit also helped to stimulate German links with British advanced industrial techniques. The entries within his diary for his visit to the Brighton Pavilion, for example, include[3]:

First we saw the kitchen and found everything excellent pertaining to cooking by steam. There is a table with an iron tabletop, steam heated, to keep the dishes hot; also cauldrons with double walls, again for letting steam into the cavity, and with stop-cocks to drain off the condensation water.

He was obviously more interested in technological innovation than in the stylistic architecture of the Pavilion.

Schinkel's visit to Britain also helped to formulate his ideas about neo-classicism which, with its reliance on uncompromised Platonic forms, was to contribute to the make-up of the Modern Movement. Schinkel's formulation of neo-classicism was influenced by the English non-stylistic industrial buildings. He refers in his diary to a visit to the Watts and Bolton iron works[4]:

> The enormous masses of buildings built of red brick by the contractor without any thought of architecture make a most uncanny impression.

This impression is caught in his sketch of the mills at Manchester (Figure 1.18).

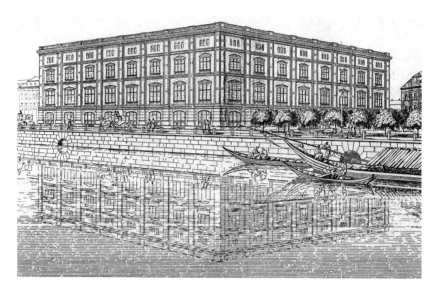

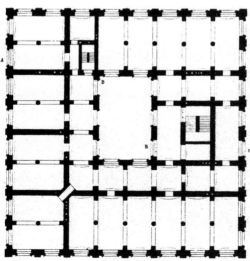

Figure 6.1 Bauakademie, Berlin, 1835; Karl Friedrich Schinkel, courtesy of Princeton Architectural Press

Schinkel's visit to Britain led him to a series of neo-classical designs which reflect the functional and industrial values that he had seen in the mills in Manchester[5]. A direct connection can be made between the box shape and frame construction of the industrial mills and his resolute design of the Bauakademie (Building Academy), Berlin, 1835[4] (Figure 6.1).

The roots of neo-classicism from Boullée, Gilly and Durand were thus developed through Schinkel's interest in the construction of industrial mills into a forceful architectural statement. The earlier rhetoric of Platonic solids was given the constructional reality of skeleton and skin.

The link between the constructional methods used in Britain and the Modern Movement can also be traced through the architect Gottfried Semper. Reference was made in Chapter 2 to his visit to the Crystal Palace in 1852. It was this visit to the Exhibition which led him to write the essay *Wissenschaft, Industrie und Kunst* (Science, Industry and Art), in which he examined the impact of industrialization and mass consumption on art and architecture. Although this essay was written to address predominantly social issues, it also foretold the influence of industrial production on constructional techniques and thus on the appearance of buildings and consumer goods. He was scornful of the movements in Britain to return to pre-industrial craft-based attitudes[6].

Another important visit to Britain, which helped to forge the links between the forthright construction of industrial buildings and the generative use of construction in the buildings of the Modern Movement, was by the German architect Hermann Muthesius. Muthesius was sponsored by the Imperial German Government to investigate English buildings. This led to his attachment to the Imperial Embassy in London for the seven years between 1897 and 1904. Muthesius's investigation led to the three-volume *Das Englische Haus* in which he portrays interesting and important characteristics of English architecture of the time. The architectural historian Julius Posener describes this[7]:

In England he met a theory, a mood may be a better word. . . . This was anti-Italian, anti-Renaissance, it was in favour of an architecture related to life, to modern life, more precisely . . .

When Muthesius described Shaw's houses as 'foundation stones of a new architecture' and his windows as reflecting 'the essence of the house', he recognized in the English country house the philosophy of functionalism.

The term 'English free architecture', which is often used to describe this period of domestic building, should not be misinterpreted to imply an architecture which was random or without control. Although 'English free architecture' was moving towards a freer position, by loosening its connections with the rigidity of the Renaissance, it was simultaneously taking on a new controlling rigour to do with the honesty with which the function of the building was expressed through its plan and form, and the honesty with which the materials and type of construction were used. Muthesius, in describing Shaw's houses, hints at this functional, rather than stylistic, approach[8]:

> In the English house one would look in vain for the kind of pomposity, for the style written with a capital 'S' which we, in Germany, are still devoted to. It is already forty years since the movement against imitation of styles began in England. It has been inspired by simple buildings in the country; and in its course it has already yielded splendid results. Let us learn from it.

Muthesius did learn from it, and through Muthesius it was implanted into Germany.

At this time a less direct, but equally important, link was being made between Britain and central Europe. This was through a group of designers who formed the Secessionist Group in Vienna. They were interested in the design implications of British machines and industry, they admired the ethical honesty and the reduction of ornament in the objects of the Arts and Crafts Movement, and they followed with interest the rationality, the use of flat planes and geometric abstraction in the work of Charles Rennie Mackintosh. Van der Velde extolled these features in his lectures in Vienna between 1893 and 1900, and Otto Wagner referred to them in his Inaugural Lecture for his appointment in 1894 as Professor of Architecture at the Akademie der Bildende Kunste. These ideas influenced the work of many of the Secessionist Group of designers in Vienna and are demonstrated in Otto Wagner's Post Office Savings Bank, Vienna, of 1905. The Banking Hall (Figure 6.2) shows a clear distinction between the expressed structure and the unadorned and well-disciplined glazing. His understanding of the fundamental use of materials is also seen on the outside of the building (Figure 6.3), where the use of thin sheets of stone as a veneer cladding is honestly demonstrated by the expressed aluminium fixings. The building also represents one of the earliest architectural uses of aluminium in the columns and roof of the entrance canopy.

Aluminium was not considered as a building material at this time. Although the existence of aluminium had first been established by Sir

Figure 6.2 Interior of the banking hall, Post Office Savings Bank, Vienna, 1905; Otto Wagner (photograph Bastiaan Valkenburg)

Humphrey Davy in 1807, it was not manufactured until Paul Heroult and Charles Hall, working independently, each discovered in 1890 a suitable flux for its production. It was not until the beginning of the twentieth century that it became used regularly in buildings.

The final connection between Britain and Germany to be considered was that made by Peter Behrens, who toured England and Scotland during 1903. Behrens was a painter by training, but from about 1898 spent much of his time as an industrial designer working on both industrial objects and exhibitions. His interest in the principles of design, rather than imposed style, led him in 1901 to organize some design courses for established craftsmen in Nuremburg. In 1902, through the influence of Muthesius, he was appointed director of the Kunstgewerbeschule (School of Arts and Crafts) in Dusseldorf, and in this capacity, and under Muthesius's guidance, he toured from London to Glasgow in 1903. It is interesting to note that, as his guided tour directed him to Glasgow, he and Muthesius must have seen both the work of Charles Rennie Mackintosh[9] and the innovatory use of metal and glass in the seminal 'curtain wall' fronts of the department

Figure 6.3 The main entrance, Post Office Savings Bank, Vienna, 1905; Otto Wagner (reproduced from *Sketches, Projects and Executed Buildings by Otto Wagner*, courtesy of Ernst Wasmuth Verlag GmbH and Co)

stores referred to in Chapter 4. Peter Behrens wrote to Muthesius on 9 August 1903[10]:

> I feel that I am sincerely indebted to you, now and forever, for all the interesting things I saw and experienced in England and Scotland. As I have already said to you, this journey has brought me to really consolidate and confirm my conception of a modern culture.

A corporate interest in the new attitude towards design was beginning to emerge in Germany at the beginning of the twentieth century. This was aided by Muthesius, who, on his return to Germany in 1904, used his influence and position as Superintendent of the Prussian Board of Trade for Schools of Arts and Crafts to speak out against the moribund imitation of historical styles which was still in use in Germany. His public lecture in 1907 stimulated controversial debate, and out of this debate came the influential group of like-minded persons who joined together to form, and privately fund, the important Deutscher Werkbund. The group consisted of craft manufacturers, industrial designers and architects; their objectives were, as recorded in *Funfzig Jahre Deutscher Werkbund* (on the history of the Werkbund)[11]:

> Selecting the best representatives of art, industry, craft, and trades, of combining all efforts towards high quality and industrial work, and of forming a rallying point for all those who were able and willing to work for high quality.

While the Werkbund had common ground with the Arts and Crafts Movement in England, it is the difference between them which proves decisive in placing the Modern Movement in Germany rather than England. The similarity lay in the common belief in a new integrity and quality; the difference lay in the method of achieving these objectives. The Arts and Crafts Movement required an enoblement of the craftsman and, through this quality of life, saw manufacturing in terms of a return to hand-craft production. The Deutscher Werkbund saw the potential of power and quality in the use of industrial machines for mass production. Julius Posener points out that, as early as 1901, Muthesius was advocating a machine aesthetic[12]:

> Let the human mind think of shapes the machine can produce. Such shapes, once they are logically developed in accordance with what machines can do, we may certainly call artistic. They will satisfy, because they will no longer be imitations of handicraft, but typically machine made shapes.

William Lethaby in England realized the significance of what was going on in Germany. He wrote in 1922 about modern German architecture and what we may learn from it, referring with some scorn to Muthesius's visit to England[13]:

> The first thing in the arts which we should learn from Germany is how to appreciate English originality. . . . All the architects who at that time did any building were investigated, sorted, tabulated and, I must say, understood.

Because the Germans 'understood' the possibilities of production and the aesthetic consequence of industrialization they were able to apply it sooner, and with more rigour, than other countries.

One of the moves towards realization of the Werkbund objectives, particularly in terms of industry, was by Peter Behrens in the work he carried out for the Allgemeine Elektricitäts-Gesellschaft (AEG) industrial company. Behrens' letter to Muthesius of 1903 clarifies his thoughts about the teaching of design. He made it clear that priority would be given to what he called 'der fortschreitenden produktiven Kunst' (the practical application of art to real problems) without which, he wrote, 'grey theory' would maintain its 'dreary domination'[14]. He realized that it could only be through the harsh reality of selecting materials and selecting a process of construction that one could achieve the actuality of design. His commissions from the AEG gave him the testing opportunity of fulfilling these ambitions.

The newspaper *Berliner Tageblatt* reported on 29 August 1907 an interview with Peter Behrens on his appointment as artistic adviser to AEG[15]:

> From now on the tendency of our age should be followed and a manner of design established appropriate to machine production. This will not be achieved through the imitation of handcraftsmanship, of other materials and of historical styles.

This is certainly a different opinion to that of Ruskin in England.

AEG, under the progressive leadership of its Managing Director, Emil Rathenau, had become a fast-growing international company. It was modern, and dealt in all things required for the new wonder of electricity. Peter Behrens' first commission in 1907 was to produce a new design for the arc light. A forerunner of the filament lamp which we use today. Edison and Swan produced the first electric light in 1879 and electric lighting began to take preference over gas lighting early in the 1890s: electricity was therefore still a new field of design. Peter Behrens' solution was not revolutionary but, through a careful reduction in the number of joints and a sensitive attention to the curvature of the reflector, he produced a successful and marketable product.

In 1907 Behrens moved to Neubabelsberg, near Potsdam, and set up a studio where, in the following year, he took on Adolf Meyer, then aged 27, Mies van der Rohe aged 22, and Walter Gropius aged 25, who had just completed his training as an architect. In 1908 Behrens carried out several exhibition contracts for AEG and in 1909 he received the important commission to construct a large new production hall for the manufacture of electric turbines.

Behrens used construction for this new Turbine Hall at Moabit, Berlin (Figure 6.4) in the same forthright manner as German industrialists were using the machine. The Hall, 207 metres long and 39 metres wide, is formed from a skeleton of 22 steel main frames placed at 9 metre centres. These main frames support not only the roof and cladding of the building but also the rails for the two 50 tonne gantry cranes.

Behrens' article, *The Turbine Hall of the AEG, Berlin*, writen in 1910, clarifies his intention[16]:

The dominant architectural idea in the design of the main hall was to pull the steel components together, and not, as is characteristic of normal lattice

Figure 6.4 AEG Turbine Hall, Berlin, 1909; Peter Behrens

construction, to spread them out. The internal volume thereby was to be contained on all sides within closed, flat planes in order to create the clarity of architectural proportions.

Externally, Behrens differentiates the structural and the non-loadbearing elements by sloping back the non-loadbearing infill parts of the fabric while retaining a vertical posture for the steel structure. Through this device he achieves, in the long side elevations, a successful contrast between the strength of the structural columns and the fragile and detached quality of the glass infilling panels. These elevations in particular allude to the industrial stimulus. The strong cadence between steel and glass, the riveted detailing of the stanchions, and the expressive cast hinge pin stanchion bearings (Figure 6.5), thought necessary at the time for movement in the frames, all link the image of massive power with cool rationality[17].

This rationality is, however, less clear on the main Huttenstrasse facade. Behrens' notion that the grooved concrete corner walls could be read both as bastions to support a representational classical pediment and simultaneously as non-loadbearing panels is optimistic. It is questionable whether such an intellectual ambiguity could be successfully translated from the abstract into the actuality of the materials and construction.

It is known that Peter Behrens, trained as he was as an industrial designer, valued and used the architectural expertise of Walter Gropius during the design and construction of the AEG Turbine Hall. Gropius in fact worked in Behrens' office for a short period in 1908

Figure 6.5 Base of the stanchion, AEG Turbine Hall, Berlin, 1909; Peter Behrens (photograph James Strike)

before setting up his own practice. He continued to collaborate with Behrens during the building of the AEG project, and this experience gave Gropius the necessary stimulus, practical experience and confidence to move forward to achieve, two years later in 1911, an even clearer synthesis of the Modern Movement. This was the construction of the Fagus factory at Alfeld-an-der-Leine (Figure 6.6). Gropius, writing in 1935 in *The New Architecture and the Bauhaus* recalls[18]:

> In 1908, when I finished my preliminary training and embarked on my career as an architect with Peter Behrens, the prevalent conceptions of architecture and architectural education were still entirely dominated by the academic stylisticism of the classical 'Orders'. It was Behrens who first introduced me to logical and systematical co-ordination in the handling of architectural problems. In the course of my active association with important schemes on which he was then engaged, and frequent discussions with him and other prominent members of the Deutscher Werkbund, my own ideas began to crystallize as to what the essential nature of building ought to be. I became obsessed by the conviction that modern constructional technique could not be denied expression in architecture, and that that expression demanded the use of unprecedented forms.

Credit must be given to Karl Benscheidt for selecting Walter Gropius to improve the image of the factory which he was having built for the manufacture of shoe-lasts. Design drawings had already been produced by the architect Edward Werner but Benscheidt had reservations. Although the foundations were already in place when Gropius was approached, he was able to overcome this restriction and turn the design into an influential example of the Modern Movement.

What makes the Fagus factory significant? To explore this question it is necessary to look at the construction of the elevations for the main three-storey block. Werner's original design for these elevations was a series of brick piers between which were thick window mullions with arched tops crossed by brick panels at each floor level. The appearance was of a predominantly solid facade with three separate windows to each floor level repeated in every bay. Gropius was looking for a building which expressed the modern industrial spirit, the modern use of materials and construction, and a modern attitude towards light and air for the industrial workers.

It is now difficult to imagine how innovative the Fagus factory must have appeared in 1911. Gropius writes in *The New Architecture and the Bauhaus*[19]:

> A breach has been made with the past, which allows us to envisage a new aspect of architecture corresponding to the technical civilization of the age we live in; the morphology of dead styles has been destroyed; and we are returning to

Figure 6.6 Fagus Factory, Alfeld-an-der-Leine, 1911; Walter Gropius and Adolf Meyer (courtesy of the British Architectural Library, RIBA, London)

honesty of thought and feeling. The general public, formerly profoundly indifferent to everything to do with building, has been shaken out of its torpor.

Gropius reduced the elevations to 'mere screens stretched between the upright framework to keep out rain, cold and noise'[17]. To achieve a clear sense of separation between the diaphanous glass skin and the upright structure, he brought the plane of the glass forward in relation to the piers so that, when seen from an angle, the glass wall obscures the piers and gives the structure a recessed and subservient appearance. Gropius produced a sense of transparency at the ends of the building by continuing the window wall past the end pier to form a clear glazed corner. The staircase within the corner bay is set close to the window wall but it never touches. This creates a 'dematerialization of the structure'[17]. The curtain wall is formed using simple, thin metal glazing section; in spite of the fact that black metal sheets are incorporated to cover the floor slabs, the curtain wall maintains the appearance of a continuous transparent plane around the building. The building is so transparent at the corners as to read as planes rather than surfaces. Gropius achieves a building which is a pure geometric prism totally devoid of ornament[20].

The Deutscher Werkbund Exhibition at Cologne in 1914 was an occasion for self-examination by its members. The papers presented, which included *Propositions* by Muthesius and *Counter Propositions* by Van de Velde, raised fundamental questions about industry, design, standardization and 'good taste'. However, it is clear from the lecture *The Task of the Werkbund in the Future*, given by Muthesius, that they recognized that a new style had emerged[21]:

... the present exhibition is certainly a fair reflection of the breadth of influence our movement has acquired ... its success has shown that commercial circles as a whole and the great majority of industrial manufacturers definitely wish to collaborate with us today.

... there can no longer be any doubt that a unified expression of style has already been achieved.

7 Towards an expressive use of concrete, 1900–1935

This chapter traces developments in the use of structural reinforced concrete between 1900 and 1935. It considers the new opportunities which these developments gave to designers and, in particular, their influence on the Expressionist Movement.

Chapter 3 traced the advent of concrete in building construction. It concluded with reference to the Weaver and Company Mill at Swansea, where, in 1898, François Hennebique made a seminal contribution to the design potential of reinforced concrete.

The Paris Exhibition of 1900 provided a useful opportunity for experiment with reinforced concrete. The structural limits of its use were explored through several futuristic structures which, like Hennebique's Palais des Lettres, Sciences et Arts (Figure 7.1), showed an eager, yet uncertain, attempt to find a new design language for reinforced concrete. In spite of several failures and accidents during the construction of some of the more adventurous pavilions, the exhibition gave an influential promotion to the use of reinforced concrete. Both Hennebique and Coignet were awarded Gold Medals for their advancement of concrete technology.

The Apartment Block in the Rue Franklin, Paris (Figure 7.2), by the engineer Auguste Perret in 1903, was one of the earliest occasions where structural concrete contributed to the visual appearance of a domestic building. Although the expressed concrete frame is limited to straight grid lines similar to a steel frame, and is also faced with ceramic tiling, nevertheless the working of the structural frame is clearly evident, particularly in the cantilevered frame for the projecting bays.

The Jahrhunderthalle (Centenary Hall) in Breslau (now Wroclaw, Poland), 1911–13, was built by Max Berg, then city architect. This building (Figure 7.3)[1] shows how the engineering characteristics of reinforced concrete developed quickly at the beginning of the

Figure 7.1 Concrete structure, Palais des Lettres, Sciences and Arts, Paris Exhibition, 1900; François Hennebique (reproduced from *Cité Industrielle*, Tony Garnier, published by Studio Vista, courtesy of Macmillan Inc)

twentieth century. The vast hall demonstrates a heavy, yet excitingly curvilinear, modern structure. Its size, 67 metres in diameter, was bigger by half than the Pantheon in Rome, which remains even today the largest masonry dome [2]. The choice of reinforced concrete was, in the words of Berg and Trauer, the building's engineers, 'to ensure that it would bear witness to the culture of our time even after the passage of centuries' [3]. The monumental scale of the exposed, shutter-marked concrete structure makes this an innovatory and important building.

While the interior of the Jahrhunderthalle is predominantly a structural statement, it shows, particularly in the shaping of its parts (Figure 7.4), how the appearance coincides with the language being explored by the architectural movement which became known as Expressionism. There is at Breslau a sense of fluidity inherent in the well-resolved use of reinforced concrete. The interior of the building

Figure 7.2 Apartment block, Rue Franklin, Paris, 1903; August Perret (courtesy of the Architectural Press photographic library)

demonstrates that reinforced concrete could produce the plastic shapes being explored in the Expressionist Movement. It was able to translate the visions of the artist into the reality of architecture.

Otto Kahtz, the artist and architect, speculated in 1909 about the motive potential of unknown building materials. He wrote in *Gedanken über Architektur, Berlin*:

> It is highly possible that later generations will achieve such mastery of materials and technique that they will construct a building or a landscape for no other purpose than that of contemplation, simply out of a desire to create in a particular mood.

His expressionist drawings[3] capture the spirit of the time. The Jahrhunderthalle represents an early step in the mastery of reinforced concrete to achieve what Otto Kahtz could only feel for in the force and plasticity of his drawings.

The Expressionist Movement was spurred on by the restlessness and distortion of World War I, which led such exponents as Erich

Figure 7.3 Jahrhunderthalle, Breslau, 1911–13; Max Berg

Figure 7.4 Internal view of structure, Jahrhunderthalle, Breslau, 1911–13; Max Berg

Mendelsohn to question the value of the neat and tidy boxes produced by the Werkbund. He criticized the members of the Bauhaus Group as having 'rectilinear minds'[4]. Mendelsohn's Einstein Tower at Potsdam became an important stimulant in the growth of Expressionist architecture, and assists in understanding the interaction between the development of structural concrete and the language of the Expressionist Movement. The emotive language of the Movement is seen in the bold yet sensuous lines of Mendelsohn's early sketches for the tower which he produced in the trenches of the Russian Front in 1917 (Figure 7.7). These powerful images need to be considered alongside the theories which he was defining at the time, for it is within these theories that Mendelsohn's self-imposed need to work with the

Figure 7.5 Esder Clothing Factory, Paris, 1919; Auguste Perret (reproduced from *Sir Owen Williams 1890–1969*, David Cottam, courtesy of the Architectural Association)

reality of construction can be identified. Mendelsohn speaks of the need [4]:

> . . . to express it in solid terms is the task, but I am glad to be subject to its law because it is its truest life.

This search for a true expression of the nature of reinforced concrete is also seen in Tony Garnier's vision of a new city, *Une Cité Industrielle*, which he wrote in 1917. He advocates the use of reinforced concrete for all the important buildings of the Cité Industrielle [5]:

> The simpler the moulds, the easier will be the construction, and consequently less the cost. This simplicity of means leads logically to a great simplicity of expression in the structure. Let us note also that, if our structure remains simple, unadorned, without moulding, bare, we are then best able to arrange the decorative arts so that each object of art will remain its purest and clearest expression because it will be totally independent of the construction. Besides, who would not see that the use of such materials results in the obtaining of the horizontals and verticals that are proper to give to the construction that calm and equilibrium that will harmonize with the lines of nature.

August Perret advanced the reality of reinforced concrete. His structure for the Esder Clothing Factory in Paris of 1919 (Figure 7.5) demonstrates, in its lightness, the material's strength. At Notre Dame, Le Raincy, of 1922–3 (Figure 7.6) he shows the natural expression of concrete straight from the shutter.

Although Mendelsohn's influential sketches for the Einstein Tower were produced in 1917, the project was not built until 1921 (Figure 7.8) and it was partly constructed in rendering over structural masonry rather than *in-situ* concrete. The tower represents everything inherent

Figure 7.6 Notre Dame, Le Raincy, 1922–3; Auguste Perret (photograph Bastiaan Valkenburg)

Figure 7.7 Sketch for the Einstein Tower, Potsdam, 1917; Erich Mendelsohn

Figure 7.8 Einstein Tower, Potsdam, 1921; Erich Mendelsohn

within the 'jellymould' characteristics of a cast concrete building, but the builders had no previous experience of constructing anything like it, and shipwrights had to be called in to tackle the complex shuttering required to form the double curved surfaces. However, it *was* made into reality and became an influential piece of architecture.

The issues are summarized in Mendelsohn's three theories, which he entitled 'the Dynamic Condition, the Rhythmic Condition and the Static Condition' [4]. The first and second theories deal with plasticity and the shape of a building. Mendelsohn refers to:

the movement of space to visualize its linear elements by means of its contour

and

to visualize the relation of the masses by means of the projection of the surfaces.

This awareness of the planar quality in the surface of a building, and the attention to the curvilinear and three-dimensional movement of its parts, is explicit in the topological modelling of Mendelsohn's Einstein Tower.

Curvilinear movement is recognizable in the concrete structure of the Airship Hangars built at Orly by Eugène Freyssinet in 1921

Figure 7.9 Airship Hangar, Orly, Paris, 1921; Eugène Freyssinet (reproduced from *Sir Owen Williams 1890–1969*, David Cottam, courtesy of the Architectural Association)

Figure 7.10 Goetheaneum II, 1923; Rudolf Steiner (photograph Bastiaan Valkenburg)

(Figure 7.9). Each shed is formed in 80 mm thick corrugated concrete shells over a 63 metre span. The surface modelling and the 'jellymould' characteristic of cast concrete were first exploited in 1923 by Rudolf Steiner for the building of Goetheanum II (Figures 7.10 and 7.11). Here the visual power of cast concrete is evident, although the structure remains inert and massive.

By this time a lighter and more refined constructional technique for concrete was being used, with the result that the expressive characteristics of the curved members changed. J. J. P. Oud demonstrates this in the thin curved canopy, supported by thin columns, at the entrance to the workers' housing at Tweede Scheepsvaart-straat, Hook of Holland, 1924–7 (Figure 7.12). Similar lightness is apparent in the spacious and open structure of the Pavilion A1 at Brno in Czechoslovakia, 1928, by Jaroslav Valenta (Figure 7.13).

By 1930 concrete technology had advanced to a position where it gave immense freedom to the designer. Aiding this freedom was the use of flat slab construction, which had been developed in America during the 1920s and transferred across the Atlantic by the Trussed Concrete Steel Company[6]. It was a time when the Modern Movement was reaching maturity and the influence of reinforced concrete became evident in the pilotis, floating white structural planes,

Figure 7.11 Interior detail, Goetheaneum II, 1923; Rudolf Steiner (photograph Bastiaan Valkenburg)

long horizontal openings and graceful ramps and staircases which typify the period. Examples of this are the Villa Savoie, Poissy, of 1929–31, by Charles-Edouard Jeanneret, known as Le Corbusier (Figures 7.14 and 7.15), and the Penguin Pool at London Zoo by

Figure 7.12 Workers' housing, Tweede Scheepsvaart Straat, Hook of Holland, 1924–7; J. J. P. Oud (photograph Bastiaan Valkenburg)

Figure 7.13 Pavilion A1, Brno, Czechoslovakia, 1928; Jaroslav Valenta (reproduced from *Building Design*, 20 November 1981)

Figure 7.14 Villa Savoie, Poissy, Paris, 1929–31; Le Corbusier (photograph Bastiaan Valkenburg)

Figure 7.15 Spiral staircase, Villa Savoie, Poissy, Paris, 1929–31; Le Corbusier (photograph Bastiaan Valkenburg)

Figure 7.16 The Penguin Pool, London Zoo, 1934 (refurbished in 1987 by Avanti Architects); Berthold Lubetkin and Tecton (photograph John Allan, courtesy of Avanti Architects)

Figure 7.17 D10, Dry Process Building, Boots Factory, Beeston, Nottingham, 1930–2; Sir Owen Williams (reproduced from *Sir Owen Williams 1890–1969*, David Cottam, courtesy of the Architectural Association)

Lubetkin, 1934 (Figure 7.16). Both demonstrate curved concrete ramps and refined flat planes of concrete to create abstract compositions.

Although many of the early experiments in concrete took place in England, little of its architectural development occurred in England until the 1930s. Owen Williams used the structural characteristics of reinforced concrete for the D10 Boots Factory, Beeston, 1930–2 (Figure 7.17). Through the controlled use of column, mushroom and thin cantilevered slab, this is a simple yet powerful design. The building also represents an early example of a patent glazing system made up from simple standard sections (Figure 7.18) and it is interesting to note how Williams makes a disciplined articulation between the planes of the glazing and the structural concrete. This is again demonstrated by Owen Williams's *Daily Express* building, Fleet Street, 1929–31 (Figure 7.19), where the structure makes pertinent use of the strengths of reinforced concrete and the whole flowing shape of the concrete structure is sheathed with a new material, black vitrolite [7].

It was, however, on the Continent that the use of structural concrete reached its greatest potential through some beautifully delicate and balanced feats of engineering. It is in this sense of balance that the beauty of these structures lies. It is the concept of balance which forms

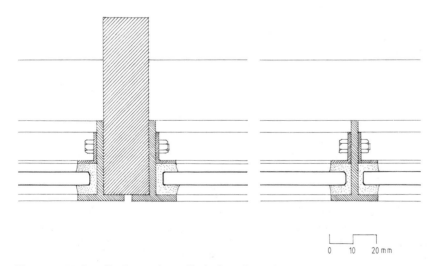

0   10   20 mm

Figure 7.18 Detail of curtain wall glazing, D10, Dry Process Building, Boots Factory, Beeston, Nottingham, 1930–2; Sir Owen Williams (drawing James Strike)

the third of Mendelsohn's theories referred to earlier. The theory titled 'the Static Condition' states[4]:

> The equalization of movement, to visualize this as elements of construction by means of ground plan and section

> Dynamic masses are shown so that their dynamism is clearly expressed so that movement and counter-movement show the balance

Figure 7.19 The *Daily Express* Building, Fleet Street, London, 1929–31; Sir Owen Williams (reproduced from *Sir Owen Williams 1890–1969*, David Cottam, courtesy of the Architectural Association)

According to the way it is built up, this mass can be mighty oppressive or finely and sensitively outlined without losing its stability.

Mendelsohn is talking predominantly about a visual sense of balance in the appearance of a building. 'Equalization of movement', 'stability' and 'balance' become the key issues in the development of reinforced concrete. Mendelsohn realized that it must be in the actual mass and structure of the building that this design balance has to exist. It is the striving for this sense and vision of structural balance that drove the great structural engineers of the period towards more daring and sinuous structures.

Mario Salvadori, civil engineer, architect, mathematician and Professor of Engineering at Columbia University, describes this awareness in his foreword to *Structures* by Pier Luigi Nervi. He describes Nervi[8]:

A mind as alert as his realized immediately that the potentialities of a new material were bound to create the need for a new approach to structural design. A greater freedom of forms . . . the use of the plastic properties of concrete . . . a fresh outlook. This new material he uses (ferro-cemento) in such an imaginative way as to open up unforeseen possibilities.

Figure 7.20 Giovanni Berta Stadium, Florence, 1930–2; Pier Luigi Nervi (reproduced from *The Works of Pier Luigi Nervi*, Nervi and Rogers, courtesy of Architectural Press)

Progressive change was due primarily to the work of Pier Luigi Nervi. He was able to see the limitations which the existing arithmetic calculations were imposing on design solutions. He realized that reinforced concrete had greater potential, and wrote[9]:

> My teacher of structures at the University of Bologna was one of the few theoreticians I have known capable of understanding the limitations of his own theories. I remember in 1913 his reading to us the alarmed letters of his German colleagues, who proved mathematically that the Risorgimento Bridge in Rome was in immediate danger of failing – and in fact should have failed already.

This was the time when the importance of the redistribution of stress in concrete was first being recognized. Nervi wrote[10]:

> The behaviour of concrete under load was more closely analysed. It was found that, particularly in its early stages, concrete flows plastically, and it was realized that this complex phenomenon allows the adjustment of concrete to a new statical condition.

This understanding of the behaviour of elasticity in structural concrete enabled Nervi to achieve the full potential of the cantilever. This led

Figure 7.21 External staircase, Giovanni Berta Stadium, Florence, 1930–2; Pier Luigi Nervi (reproduced from *Sir Owen Williams 1890–1969*, David Cottam, courtesy of the Architectural Association)

him to such designs as the Giovanni Berta Stadium at Florence, 1930–2, where the cross-sections (Figure 7.20) show the poise and balance of the structure and the elegant external staircases (Figure 7.21) demonstrate the inherent aesthetic of reinforced concrete.

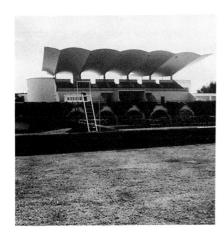

Figure 7.22 Spectator stand, Madrid Racecourse, 1935; Eduardo Torroja (reproduced from *The Structures of Eduardo Tarroja*, Eduardo Tarroja)

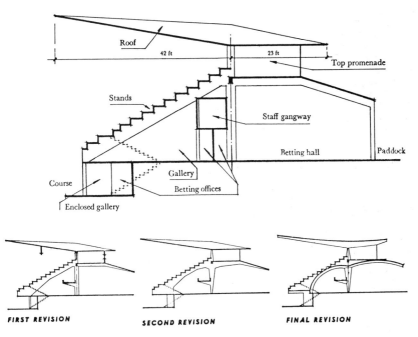

Figure 7.23 Development sections, spectator stand, madrid Racecourse, 1935; Eduardo Torroja (reproduced from *The Structures of Eduardo Tarroja*, Eduardo Tarroja)

This understanding of the structural behaviour of reinforced concrete, and its design characteristics, are again demonstrated in the work of the Spanish engineer Eduardo Torroja. The sketches produced during the development of the design for the spectator stand at the Madrid racecourse, 1935 (Figures 7.22 and 7.23), show his awareness of the structural elasticity and natural strength of certain shapes in concrete, and provided routes for him through the design process. The scheme is progressively refined by taking away redundant structure as it develops towards an economic, structural and visual balance. In his autobiography Torroja describes the synthesis of this design process and concludes with the question[11]:

> Is the invention of an especially adapted form to solve a specific problem strictly an imaginative process, or is it the result of logical reasoning based on technical training? I do not think it is either of the two, but rather both together. The imagination alone could not have reached such a design unaided by reason, nor could a process of deduction, advancing by successive cycles of refinement, have been so logical and determinate as to lead inevitably to it.

8 Development of building systems and industrialization during the inter-war period

This chapter identifies the most significant change to take place within the building industry during the inter-war period as being the general industrialization of the industry and the development of industrialized building systems. It traces the growth of building systems in Britain and also considers the more conceptual thinking about systems which took place on the Continent. It explores the effect of industrialization on the attitude of designers towards architectural design.

The terms used to describe industrialized building are difficult to define as their meanings vary according to the circumstance of their use; however, the central techniques include prefabrication, transportation and mass-production. While it is generally accepted that industrialized building belongs to the twentieth century, it is important to note that these individual techniques have been used in their own separate way throughout history; they are in themselves not new.

What then are the distinctive features of the industrialized buildings which developed during the period between the two World Wars? It was not the invention of prefabrication, or transportation or mass-production, as these had existed for years; it was not even their coming together, since Paxton, for example, had used them collectively for the building of the Crystal Palace. The significance was that during the inter-war period these techniques were consciously brought together to produce a form of construction designed, not for a single specific building, but as a system of factory-based assembly-line components which could be transported to the different sites to produce similar buildings.

Before looking at the inter-war developments, it is therefore necessary to consider what had evolved prior to that period. Examples of the separate constituent parts of industrialized building can be found in most periods of history, and a review of each will help to identify its own particular characteristic and role within the evolutionary process. These early examples set up a chain of events which led gradually to a change of attitude away from the precedence of conventional and traditional construction.

An impressive use of the transportation of building parts took place as early as the second century BC for the building of Stonehenge. Late Neolithic man arranged for the blue stones, each weighing about 2 tonnes, to be moved by means of rollers and river raft from the Preseli Hills, Dyfed, to the site on the Wiltshire Plain[1]. This gargantuan task, driven by religious fervour and power, illustrates that it has always been possible to move large and heavy building parts over long distances if the effort, in terms of manpower, time and transport, is considered necessary to achieve the prestige, convenience or speed required for a particular building project.

An early example of prefabrication is the roof of the Chapel Royal at Hampton Court Palace. The construction in 1535 of the new carved and decorated timber vault roof required large baulks of oak, which were available from the forests around the village of Sonning on the Thames near Reading. Henry VIII wanted best-quality workmanship and wanted it in a hurry. It was resolved that this could be achieved by forming and carving the roof on the ground at Sonning. While this required a great deal of organization, it was successful and the completed roof was shipped in sections by barge up the Thames to Hampton, where they were hoisted into place[2].

One of the greatest periods of mass-production was in the repetitive houses built, row after row, during the expansion of the cities in the second half of the nineteenth century. Although these large estates were made up of identical, or at least very similar, houses, this was due not solely to the economic advantages of mass-production but also to the restrictive covenants which the ground landlord used to control the size and design of the houses. It was quite common for the ground landlord to sell the building rights to several contractors ranging from an enterprising bricklayer to a large established firm of contractors.

It was through the Industrial Revolution that the process of making parts of buildings in factories became recognized practice. The growth of the factory-based cast-iron industry flourished from the early nineteenth century, and it was around the iron industry that prefabrication developed. The growth of the inland waterways and the expansion of the railway system made transport of building parts feasible. By the middle of the nineteenth century the process of prefabrication was making a mark on the appearance of buildings, as is seen in the repetitive factory-cast elements that made up the Crystal Palace. However, by the turn of the century enthusiasm for prefabricated units as a generator of architecture was in decline as interest moved back towards revivalist architectural styles rather than industrial images. The engineering feat of Tower Bridge by Sir John Wolfe Barry and Sir Horace Jones in 1886–94 was covered by Gothic stonework. Similarly, the Ritz Hotel, London, by Mewes and Davis in 1903–6, the first of London's steel-frame buildings, was faced with Beaux-Arts stonework detailing.

One bright light in this period of reaction against industrialization was the isolated example of an interesting tenement block in Liverpool built using prefabricated concrete panels (Figure 8.1). This was built in 1904–5 by the City Engineer, John Alexander Brodie[3]. His report to the Housing Committee includes the following description[4]:

> The principle adopted for the construction of each room . . . has been that of a dove-tailed box – each of the four sides, the floor and ceiling . . . consisting of one concrete slab made in a mould at a depot . . . conveyed behind a traction engine to the site and erected in position.

Figure 8.1 Tenement Flats, Liverpool, 1904; J. A. Brodie (reproduced from *RIBA Journal*, June 1963, courtesy of RIBA Journal)

This represents an exceptionally early example of system building and it is regrettable that so little was recorded about the project.

It was not until the early 1920s that the idea of industrialized building systems, based on mass-produced factory prefabricated units for the construction of large numbers of repetitive and identical buildings, was given any degree of debate. The outstanding cause of this shift in attitude was the need for housing at the end of World War I.

House building having come to standstill during the war, at its end the need for housing was focused by the emotive slogan 'Homes Fit for Heroes'. The response to this is clarified by R. B. White[5]:

> . . . the history of attempts at prefabrication between the two world wars is largely a history of committee reports and of design proposals rather than of any positive developments in building technology . . . it illustrates the time lag likely to occur between the first attempts by administrators and technologists . . . to lead a traditional industry . . . into the new ways deemed to be necessary to meet an unprecedented situation.

A survey carried out in 1917 by the Local Government Board established an immediate shortage of 170 000 houses. The number of skilled craftsmen in the building trades had been in steady decline from the turn of the century; the *National Housing Manual* of 1923[6] highlighted the acute shortage of bricklayers, who had fallen in number from 116 000 in 1901 to 53 000 by 1920. There was neither the skilled labour force nor the materials to solve the housing problem by use of traditional construction. Yet, in spite of the importance and urgency of the problem, the government could not stimulate the country towards industrialized system building to solve the problem. Restrictive practices, conservative opinion, the poor state of the railways and roads, and the complex, inconsistent and intransigent procedures of Building Control all prevented the industry from gearing up for industrialized prefabrication. Most of what was built used traditional construction. The Ministry of Reconstruction publication *Reconstruction Problems*, Vol. 1, Pamphlet No. 7, 'Housing in England and Wales' stated:

> . . . that substantial financial assitance would be given to those local authorities that were prepared to carry through without delay housing for the working classes which would be approved by the Local Government Board.

It would appear that money was available for building; perhaps the population was too impatient for quick results to wait for the authorities to organize a system of industrialized building. R. B. White confirms this view[7]:

In a state of war-weariness, and of impatience to return to a 'normal' way of life, it was perhaps only too easy to blame a government for delays and shortcomings . . . labour was in no mood, after the war, to tolerate dictatorial methods that would have involved direction or an interference with the established practices agreed by the various unions.

It is, however, important to consider what successes did occur during the inter-war period.

The Tudor Walters Report of 1918, set up by the Local Government Board, brought together knowledge and expertise from the architectural and engineering professions, contractors, industrialists and other interested bodies. It provided, for the first time, a valuable and centralized view of the building industry. The Local Government Board Committee on Building Bylaws issued, in 1918, the important report *Command 9213*, which stressed the need to revise unnecessarily obstructive bylaws and the need for local authorities to bring their bylaws into line with the latest approved methods of construction. The Committee for Standardization and New Materials was set up in 1919 to co-ordinate the size of building materials and components which were, at that time, still subject to regional variation. It is regrettable that this had little immediate effect on the ingrained habits of British manufacturers, especially in comparison with the USA where, unrestricted by precedent, they were able, through such farsighted industrialists as Albert Farwell Bernis, to benefit from the new factories to mass-produce standardized materials.

Although most house building was carried out using traditional construction, even within this market scientific advancement was the key. The Department of Scientific and Industrial Research for the Board of Agriculture and Fisheries set up some experimental construction in 1919–20 for the provision of smallholder dwellings[8]. A project at Amesbury, Wiltshire, looked at the economies of various types of construction including cob, pisé de terre, concrete blocks using chalk aggregate, and, of particular interest, reinforced concrete. The concrete dwelling[9] was two storeys with *in-situ* reinforced concrete walls, a precast T-beam first floor and precast roof trusses carrying a 50-mm Pudlo waterproofing. Within this predominantly traditional market, attempts were made to start up industrialized systems. Towards this end, the government set up ten sites around the country to encourage contractors to demonstrate their particular type of system-built houses. One such site was at Acton where a limited number of concrete-framed trial houses were built[10] (Figure 8.2). Although most of these trial systems failed to make progress, a few did

Figure 8.2 Reinforced concrete-framed houses, Acton, London, 1920 (reproduced from *Prefabrication*, R. B. White, with permission of the Controller of Her Majesty's Stationery Office)

achieve a limited run of production. It is important to consider these systems, not for their financial failure but for the contribution they made to the long-term evolution of expertise in prefabrication techniques and system building.

Companies which did manage to push forward the techniques of prefabrication included those which developed the Waller System and the Dorlornco System.

The Waller System consisted of large precast concrete components (Figure 8.3). The external walls were formed using two precast, storey-height slabs separated by a 75 mm cavity. The external slab was 32 mm thick reinforced dense concrete and the inner leaf 50 mm clinker concrete. The slabs were connected at one metre intervals by 'columns' cast *in situ*, the columns being joined together at first floor level and eaves level by *in-situ* reinforced concrete beams. The roof was formed using large reinforced concrete trays which spanned from eaves to ridge. The system almost eliminated bricklayers and slaters. The total number of houses built is uncertain; one hundred were built at Poole and about fifty at Leeds[11]. The government magazine *Housing*, 16 August 1920, includes a report on the Waller System

Section through roof slab

Section through wall (in plan)

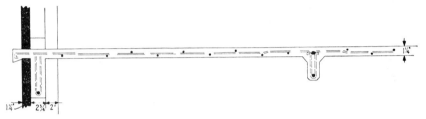

Section through floor

Figure 8.3 Waller system of house construction, 1920s (reproduced from *Prefabrication*, R. B. White, with permission of the Controller of Her Majesty's Stationery Office)

which predicted that it would need a minimum production of 500 houses to pay for the cost of setting up the precasting factory. Although the system did not become profitable it contained features which were later to be put to profitable use by other companies. It came as near to what we now mean by prefabrication as anything at that time[11].

The Dorlornco System (Figure 8.4), promoted by Messrs Dorman Long, used a steel-frame form of construction clad externally with 38-mm cement rendering over ribbed metal lathing, and lined internally with 50-mm clinker blocks with a plaster finish. The metal frame, which included the structure for the roof, was made from prepared light rolled sections which could be easily and quickly assembled on site. The first houses were built at Doncaster in 1920 and the total number finally reached about 10 000. The external rendering on many of the houses eventually failed due to corrosion of the lathing, and the external covering was often replaced with other materials. In spite of this failure the system still made an important technical step forward.

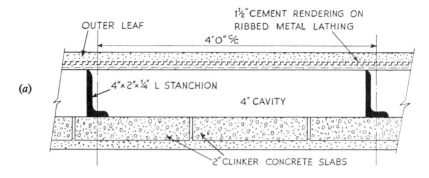

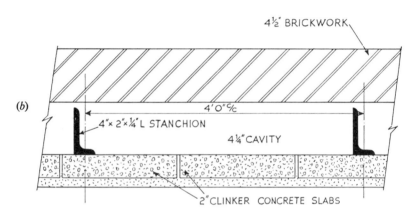

Horizontal wall sections, (a) before and (b) after conversion of external cladding to brickwork following corrosion of steel lathing and failure of rendering

Figure 8.4 Dorlornco system of house construction, 1920s (reproduced from *Prefabrication*, R. B. White, with permission of the Controller of Her Majesty's Stationery Office)

The Atholl steel house (Figure 8.5) was one of a group of prefabricated house types which made use of steel[12]. It is doubtful whether more than 3000 dwellings were constructed, certainly insufficient to cover the costs involved in factory equipment. These early attempts at steel construction and steel cladding were probably too heavy and clumsy for domestic architecture.

These British systems convey a sense of pragmatism. They appear as industrial solutions to cost, time and manufacturing problems, and while they play an important role in the evolutionary process of prefabrication, they deal only with the specific problems of production

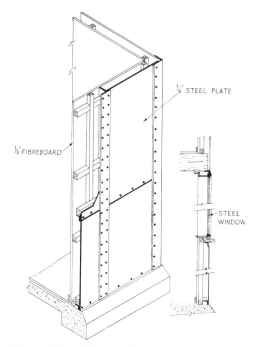

Figure 8.5 Atholl steel house (reproduced from *Prefabrication*, R. B. White, with permission of the Controller of Her Majesty's Stationery Office)

and assembly. They avoid the potential inherent within the principles of system building; it is as if they were confined to a preconceived solution based on the format of the traditional house, afraid of an unfamiliar outcome.

Capital for the large investments required for system building became progressively restricted in the mid-1920s and the industrialists therefore withdrew from system building. By about 1928, the production of system-built houses had ceased. The influence of system building did, however, continue to be part of the architectural debate. Mass housing and social concern became a key issue, particularly during the Depression of the 1930s when architects and planners looked for a better future, with architecture responding to the real needs of society[13]. *Unit One*, a publication set up by like-minded architects and artists, included an article by Wells Coates:

> What is the essential intention of the art of architecture? . . . architecture is the art of providing ordered shelter for a multitude of human activities.

The concept, albeit not the reality, of system building for rebuilding the cities played an important part in this debate and was part of the thinking behind the new Town Planning Acts which aimed to bring about an ordered future.

Although system building failed to achieve these aims during the 1930s, this striving for an architecture which represented modern Britain was achieved in a few individual projects. This is seen, for example, in the early Modern Movement houses such as Amyas Connell's 'High and Over' at Amersham, Bucks, 1929 (Figure 8.6) and 'Noah's House', on the Thames at Bourne End, 1930, where Colin Lucas first used monolithic reinforced concrete. The social concern is seen in such achievements as the Finsbury Health Centre designed by the Tecton Group in 1938.

While system building in Britain had, during the 1920s, been somewhat of a pragmatic affair, developments on the Continent had followed a more adventurous route. Although little industrialized construction was actually achieved, it evolved from a more lively debate about the fundamental design principles of industrialized systems. Industrialized building was pioneeered not by industrialists, as in Britain, but by designers who focused their thoughts on the underlying principles of system building rather than on time charts and cost margins. The two principal figures behind this striving for a clearer and more fundamental understanding of industrialization were Le Corbusier and Walter Gropius.

Figure 8.6 'High and Over', Amersham, Buckinghamshire, 1929; Amyas Connell (reproduced from Architectural Design Special Issue, *Britain in the Thirties*, photograph Herbert Felton, courtesy of Academy Group Ltd)

As early as 1914, Le Corbusier had conceived the notion of a standardized structural system for house building. The Dom-Ino houses consisted of a standard framework of reinforced concrete (Figure 8.7) which was suitable for infilling in various ways to provide different types of accommodation. The standard frames were built using reinforced concrete made without framework. Special arrangements were set up on the site to permit the pouring of absolutely smooth and level floor slabs by means of simple scaffolding of double-T beams fastened temporarily to collars fixed to the top of each column. [14]. Le Corbusier expected that the structural Dom-Ino frames would be mass-produced by one contractor and that the house would then be completed by a separate contractor using standardized window, door and partition units to produce the various plan arrangements required by each client.

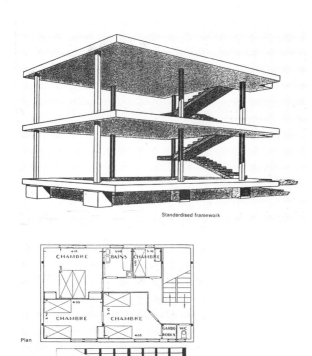

Figure 8.7 Dom-Ino house, 1914; Le Corbusier

Le Corbusier refers, in his *Five Points of a New Architecture*, to the advantages of the 'free plan'[14]:

> Reinforced concrete in the house brings about the free plan. The floors no longer superimpose rooms of the same size. They are free. A great economy of constructed volume, a rigorous use of each centimetre.

Le Corbusier extends the notion to the 'free facade'[14]:

> The facades are now only light membranes composed of insulating or window elements; the facade is free . . .

There was a sense of vitality in the air; designers and artists gathered to discuss the implications and design possibilities generated by the new industrial society. Le Corbusier was introduced in 1917 to the Swiss architect, draftsman and artist Amédée Ozenfant. The collaboration stimulated a debate about the fusion between art and industry. Ozenfant describes their time together at his Parisian atelier[15]:

> Together we read my notes on purism, and I proposed our combining ideas and friends, doing exhibitions and writing . . . The apartment was stripped of fancy ceilings and ornamentation and all walls white-washed, one of the first signs of the eliminating process in architecture which I called the 'vacuum-cleaning period' . . . we drew lessons from industrial technique dear to his master Auguste Perret and myself . . . We were enthusiastic about new bridges, sea-going liners, dams, aeroplanes. Was the expression 'purism' well chosen? For us it meant purity.

From this atelier came the influential review *L'Esprit Nouveau*. The editorial for its first publication in October 1920 proclaimed[16]:

> In industry and civil engineering, capital acquisitions announce a period of great architecture. Nobody now denies the aesthetics which are revealed by buildings of modern industry. Machines and factories show proportions, volume play and materials worthy of being called works of art.

Le Corbusier became euphoric in his enthusiasm for industrialization. He wrote about mass-production houses in 1923[17]:

> A great epoch has begun. There exists a new spirit . . . Industry, overwhelming us like a flood which rolls on towards its destined ends . . .

It continues at length in the same vein of determinist absolutes[18]. It represents Le Corbusier's ethos of machine-made housing 'machine à habiter', often incompletely translated as 'a machine to live in'.

In 1925, Le Corbusier was given the opportunity to realize his ideas when the Bordeaux industrialist M. Fruges commissioned him to build mass-produced houses at Pessac (Figure 8.8). Le Corbusier recollects his appointment[19]:

Figure 8.8 Mass-produced houses, Pessac, near Bordeaux, 1925; Le Corbusier (reproduced from *Lived-in Architecture: Pessac Revisited*, Philippe Boudon, courtesy of Lund Humphries)

> Pessac should be a laboratory. In short: I ask you to pose the problem of a house plan, of finding a method of standardization to make use of walls, floors and roofs conforming to the most rigorous requirements for strength and efficiency and lending themselves to try taylor-like methods of mass-production by use of machines which I shall authorize you to buy.

Le Corbusier's use of the words 'true taylor-like methods of mass-production' refer to his interest in 'Taylorism', the American-based scientific analysis of factory production[20]. F. W. Taylor's influential book *Principles of Scientific Organization of Factories* had been translated into French in 1912, and his ideas about the relationship between management and workers, the establishment of sequential work processes and the appropriate output per worker became part of Le Corbusier's attitude to the design of mass-produced houses.

Le Corbusier was obviously eager to prove his modern ideas about production and to show the significance of this new industrialization through his pioneering design concepts. However, his enthusiasm and his abilities were probably too advanced for the conservative attitudes of the time. Fruges had a more down to-earth approach when he commissioned Le Corbusier. Although Fruges showed considerable interest in industrialization, he saw it as a means of producing houses for homeless French soldiers after the war; he did not see it, as did Le Corbusier, as a route into new and unknown design solutions. The whole project was frustrated by their conflicting aspirations. Fruges records[21]:

> I chose Pessac, which was famous for the pure air of its pine trees, as the site for this settlement . . . I had fruit trees and ornamental shrubs planted in every garden . . . his inveterate hatred of all forms of decoration, he wanted to leave the walls completely unfinished so that they still showed the marks of the shuttering. I was flabbergasted . . . It was in vain that I asked him to put himself in the place of the purchasers, whose eyes are accustomed to decorative effects . . . The architects of Bordeaux set up a general hue and cry; they criticized everything with the result we found no purchasers for the houses.

The collaboration led to a sequence of disappointments culminating in the project being stopped when the Bordeaux authorities refused to grant permits of habitation for the fifty houses that had been completed out of the proposed two hundred. The French government fortunately attached importance to the experiment and modified legislation to allow the houses at Pessac to be inhabited at a nominal rent by families with a low income.

It is surprising, therefore, and to Le Corbusier's credit, that the houses built at Pessac managed to achieve so much progress towards industrialized building, particularly in their move towards the design potential inherent within the new methods of production. The fifty houses were built within one year, and the degree of variation, insisted on by Fruges, was achieved by the strict use of cell types which required only one type of reinforced concrete beam, 5 metres in length, and only three types of standard window.

Walter Gropius built even fewer industrialized buildings during the inter-war period than Le Corbusier. Nevertheless, his influence on the development of system building proved to be of equal importance. His influence was exerted not through the setting up of factories for mass production, nor through the masterminding of large system-built housing projects, but rather through his teaching, his experimental projects and his writing. He became director of the Bauhaus School in 1919, and it was in this capacity that he was able to stimulate debate and set up pilot projects to explore the fundamentals of system building. At the Bauhaus, he was able to introduce to the students his ideas about the new relationship between architects and industry. He wrote in *The New Architecture of the Bauhaus*[22]:

> Building, hitherto an essentially manual trade, is already in course of transformation into an organized industry. More and more work that used to be done on the scaffolding is now carried out under factory conditions far away from the site.

He pursues this theme by extolling the advantages of cost and construction techniques which are independent of wet and icy weather; he recognizes the influence of factory production on the appearance of the final article[23]:

> It is to its intrinsic particularity that each different type of machine owes the 'genuine stamp' and 'individual beauty' of its products. Senseless imitation of hand-made goods by machinery infallibly bears the mark of a makeshift substitute.

Gropius set up workshops at the Bauhaus at Weimar as laboratories for experimentation, and instigated projects to 'produce practical new designs and improved models for mass-production'[23]. These experimental projects need to be viewed within the exuberance and intensity of the discussion that was taking place at the Bauhaus. Gropius' private architects' studio was always open to interested students and became a fruitful meeting place between himself, Adolf Meyer, with whom he worked, George Muche, painter and member of the Bauhaus staff, and a group of dedicated students.

The first of these investigations, the Serial House project of 1921, set out to explore the characteristics of variability when confronted with the restraints of rationalization and standardization. Although the results of the experiments are unclear, the papers and diagrams produced portray an attempt to reach an understanding of the basic principles.

In 1926 a prototype 'Steel House' (Figure 8.9) was constructed at Torten near Dessau to coincide with the opening of the new Bauhaus

Figure 8.9 Steel House, Torten, 1926; George Muche

building at Dessau. The project was led by George Muche, with Richard Paulick from Gropius' office adding technical advice. It consisted of a concrete foundation and a steel structure infilled with a 3-mm Siemens steel external plate, insulation, an air space, torfoleum plates and plaster-slag boarding. The house is interesting for its early use of a steel structure designed to allow for flexible plan arrangements. It is interesting also for its early use of dry construction made possible by the use of the steel frame, albeit heavy by modern standards, and the early use of plasterboard which was introduced into building construction in the mid-1920s. The prefabricated system used at Torten was further developed by Gropius for two houses built for the City of Stuttgart as part of the Weissenhofsiedlung Werkbund Housing Exhibition of 1927. This project, the Kleinhaus (Figure 8.10), pursued the ideals of lightweight dry construction. Gropius reduced the weight of the external skin with asbestos board in lieu of steel plate and internally used the new materials of plywood for the walls and celotex for the ceilings. Gropius wrote[24]:

> Dry assembly offers the best prospects because moisture is the direct cause of most of the weaknesses of the old methods of building. . . . By eliminating this factor, and so assuring the perfect interlocking of all component parts, the prefabricated house makes it possible to guarantee a fixed price and a definite period of construction.

He was able to put this into practice in 1931 when he designed the Copper-Plate Houses (Figure 8.11). This was a completely industrial-

Figure 8.10 Kleinhaus, Stuttgart, 1927; Walter Gropius

Figure 8.11 Copper-Plate Houses, 1932; Walter Gropius (reproduced from *New Architecture of the Bauhaus*, Walter Gropius, courtesy of Faber and Faber)

ized system for a five-roomed house which could be produced in the factory, loaded onto a lorry, transported and dry-assembled on site. The units were manufactured in a factory on a purpose-built assembly line. The units were timber framed with insulation, fitted with glazed windows, and finished externally with sheet copper strengthened with a fine corrugation, and internally with either asbestos cement board or ribbed sheet aluminium.

In *Das Wachsende Haus*, written by Martin Wagner in the same year, 1931, Walter Gropius gives a report on the copper houses[25]:

> The fabrication of copper houses on the assembly line, according to a patent held by Forster and Kraft, was developed by me, both as to techniques and with regard to the organization of the process; this was done only after numerous tests and expert testimony from scientific institutes.

A few of these houses were built as experimental units at Finow near Berlin just before the economic collapse of Germany forced the firm to close.

The new industrialized building systems were not without their critics. There were those who saw them as dogmatic, soulless and unyielding to the designer's personal aspiration. Others took an interest in the latest schemes, not because they wished to contribute to the development of industrialization, but because they saw in them new images which they could use for a new stylistic architecture. They wanted to be seen to be modern.

Gropius was, however, aware of the dangers and wrote[26]:

> The development of the New Architecture encountered serious obstacles at a very early stage of its development. Conflicting theories and the dogmas enunciated in architects' personal manifestos all helped to confuse the main issue . . . 'modern' architecture became fashionable in several countries; with the result that formalistic imitation and snobbery distorted the fundamental truth.

This diversion of interest towards a new stylistic architecture, together with the lack of finance in the economy, meant that little was done during the 1930s towards the development of industrialized techniques.

One system which did manage to move the boundaries forward was the Mopin System, named after its originator, the French engineer Eugène Mopin. It was used in 1934–5 for a large housing scheme at Drancy near Paris (Figure 8.12). The architects were Eugène Beaudoin and Marcel Lods. The constructional system (Figure 8.13) is described in an article in 1935[27]:

> The Mopin system is carried out in three stages. (a) A light steel framework is erected. It is self-supporting, but not calculated to carry ordinary working loads. (ii) The units are fixed between the steel members to form walls. These units are pre-cast slabs of T-section, made of vibrated concrete (i.e. a specially

Figure 8.12 Housing scheme, Cité de la Muette à Drancy, Paris, 1934–5; E. Mopin with Beaudouin and Lods (reproduced from *Architect and Building News*, 15 February 1935, courtesy of the British Architectural Library, RIBA, London)

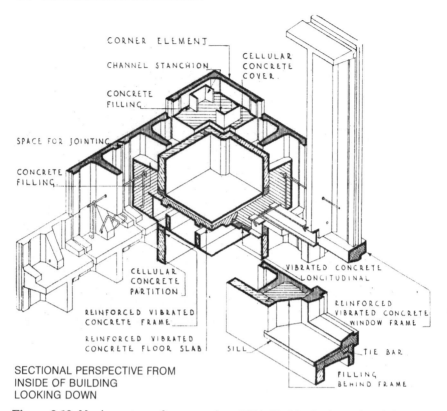

CORNER ELEMENT

CHANNEL STANCHION

CELLULAR
CONCRETE
COVER.

CONCRETE
FILLING

SPACE FOR JOINTING

CONCRETE
FILLING

CELLULAR
CONCRETE
PARTITION

REINFORCED VIBRATED
CONCRETE FRAME

REINFORCED VIBRATED
CONCRETE FLOOR SLAB

SILL

VIBRATED CONCRETE
LONGITUDINAL

REINFORCED
VIBRATED CONCRETE
WINDOW FRAME

TIE BAR

FILLING
BEHIND FRAME

SECTIONAL PERSPECTIVE FROM
INSIDE OF BUILDING
LOOKING DOWN

Figure 8.13 Mopin system of construction, 1934; E. Mopin (reproduced from *Architect and Building News*, 15 February 1935, courtesy of the British Architectural Library, RIBA, London)

dense concrete, placed on a vibrating table while in the mould) and are joined by cement pointing in the V-joint which occurs between each pair. Rods are embedded in the units and project at top and bottom, enabling their ends to be bent round the steel frame. (iii) Cellular concrete casing is fixed on the inner side of the walls and concrete is then poured in the intervening space to a certain depth at every floor level. The wall-units and inner casing act as permanent shuttering, while the steel becomes embedded in the concrete so that the building is transformed into a homogeneous reinforced concrete frame structure, with cavity walls.

The article also provides an interesting insight into the architectural debate in England in the mid-1930s:

Pre-fabrication looms large in the immediate future of architecture, for the proper solutions of its problems would in turn solve many difficulties in the realm of housing. In this country the subject has not yet been seriously tackled, partly because building regulations do not encourage the introduction of new

Figure 8.14 Quarry Hill Flats, Leeds, 1938–40; E. Mopin (reproduced from *Prefabrication*, R. B. White, with permission of the Controller of Her Majesty's Stationery Office)

Figure 8.15 On-site prefabrication of Mopin units, Quarry Hill Flats, Leeds, 1938–40; E. Mopin (reproduced from *Architectural Record*, February 1939, copyright 1939 by McGraw-Hill Inc., reproduced with the permission of the publishers)

and experimental building methods and partly because there is no system of pre-fabrication in sight which would not bring with it disadvantages like standardized plans, new building organization and inadequate insulation. There is, however, one system which has been worked out by a French engineer, M. E. Mopin, and which bears his name.

The Mopin System was used for the only large industrialized housing scheme to be built in England prior to the outbreak of World War II. This was the Quarry Hill Flats at Leeds, 1938–40 (Figure 8.14). An on-site factory was set up to prefabricate both the steel frames and the concrete panels (Figure 8.15). This achieved a 25% saving of time and 50% reduction in weight compared with other types of reinforced-concrete house construction.

Development of industrialized housing came to a halt at the outbreak of World War II.

9 Industry, art and architecture, 1920–1940

Chapter 8 looked at system building during the inter-war period. It followed its pragmatic development in Britain and observed the fundamental debate which evolved in France and Germany. This debate is now used as a starting point to explore, the connections which were being made between industry art and architecture. It explores contemporary thoughts on how each influenced the other, and how each was part of the wider interaction between industry, construction, society, and art. It explores the idea that this synthesis was a generator of modern architecture.

One of the strongest centres of the debate was the Bauhaus. Their curriculum aimed to develop the process, begun at the Weimar Academy of Arts and fostered by the Deutsche Werkbund, of freeing the student from the exacting but restricted study of existing attitudes. Their aim was to expose the students to imaginative modern artists such as Klee, Kandinsky and Oskar Schlemmer, and to encourage them to explore connections between nature, materials, construction, industry and society. Walter Gropius, Director of the Bauhaus during these formative early years[1], showed the strength of his conviction by appointing the unknown young artist Moholy-Nagy to join the Bauhaus staff. He recognized that Moholy-Nagy was prepared to confront the design issues inherent in the growth of industry and the machine[2].

The debate polarized around the images which were arising from the use of new methods for building construction. Should the new buildings, which were being constructed by the new industrialized processes, be influenced by the design theories of abstract art or should each new industrialized building technique generate, from within itself, its own distinctive and separate identity, untouched and unsullied by external artistic influences? There was, especially during the early years of the Bauhaus, an intensive search to establish ground rules which would lead to a better understanding of the design process. There was a belief that the investigations, led by such artists as Klee, Kandinsky and Moholy-Nagy, would unlock these theories. Manifestos were produced, each with an aura of fundamental truth, by Kandinsky (*Little Articles on Big Questions* of 1919) and Paul Klee (*Creative Credo* of 1920 and *Ways of Nature Study* of 1923). These, together with other publications, each contributed to the case that all design was controlled by overriding principles. Moholy-Nagy, in his text *From Materials to Architecture*[3], referred to the common creative spirit in the design of the stairs of an engine-house and the spiral supporting a sculpture, emphasized the similar qualities in easel painting and photography and in a building and a stage set, and found no clear dividing line between art and non-art.

The thought, therefore, was that industrialization and art were in some respects one and the same, that they both evolved from the same design ethos, and that an understanding of the principles would shed light on the design process for industrialized products. This would lead to an understanding of the visual grammar and identity of industrialized articles, an understanding of what the new industrialized buildings should look like.

The debate was fueled by others who held an opposing view: that art played no part whatsoever in the visual grammar of industrialized design, that industrial design was not affected by a generic abstraction of art, and that it was only within the machine and the industrial process that the new aesthetic would be found. One of the strongest voices for this view was George Muche who, in 1926, wrote the article for the Bauhaus journal *Fine Art and Industrial Form*[4]:

> The illusion that fine art must be absorbed in creative types of industrial design is destroyed as soon as it comes face to face with concrete reality. Abstract painting, which has been led with convincingly unambiguous intentions from its artistic Utopia into the promising field of industrial design, seems quite suddenly to lose its predicted significance as a form-determining element, since the formal design of industrial products that are manufactured by mechanical means follows laws that cannot be derived from the fine arts.

It was a time of intense debate, a period of shifting and complex opinions. Three particular issues, all of which centre on the design implications of industrialization, may be identified. First, a change in the attitude of the designer towards industrialization; second, recognition of the anonymous character of industrialization; and third, identification of the concept within industrial design which became labelled 'elementalism'.

The change in the attitude of designers towards industrialization needs to be seen from a broader viewpoint. The Bauhaus was not the only place where the debate was taking place. It was part of a wider international debate, with a particularly strong influence from the polemics of the Constructivist Group in Russia. The result of this debate was that the machine and the industrial process became, through progressive investigation and exposure, an accepted and respectable part of design theory.

The architectural activity of the Constructivist Group was greatly influenced by the theoretical writing of Moisei Ginsburg who, in his seminal treatise *Stil'i Epokha* (*Style and Epoch*) of 1924, set out an evocative and emotional, yet at the same time clear and reasoned, case for a change of attitude. His opening text, *Style. Elements of Architectural Style. Continuity and Independence in the Change of Styles*, recognizes the symptoms of change identifiable in the infrastructure of industry, the activity of the arts and the ideals of a socialist way of life[5]:

> If a truly modern rhythm begins to reverberate in a modern form in unison with the rhythms of labour and the joys of the present day, then naturally it will at length also have to be heard by those whose life and toil create that rhythm. It can be said that the artist's craft and any other craft will then proceed towards a single goal, and there will inevitably come a time when, finally, all these lines will intersect, i.e. when we shall discover our great style, in which the acts of creation and contemplation will become fused.

The change of attitude towards industrialization and design was also aided by the political closure of the Bauhaus in 1933, which caused many of its influential teachers to leave Germany to express and practise their belief in Western Europe and the United States.

The second issue was the recognition of the anonymous character of industrialization. In mass-production, each item produced from the machine is anonymous and impersonal with respect to each and every other unit produced. Similarly, in an estate made up, for example, of numerous Copper-Plate Houses of the 1931 system, each mass-produced front door panel would be identical on all the houses throughout the estate. Extending this to a building system which produces not only identical panels but also identical houses, the situation is reached where each house throughout the estate becomes an impersonal unit with respect to all of the other houses. This characteristic was not considered to be detrimental; it was recognized that there would be a new relationship between the designer and the object and that the phenomena of anonymity could be realized as an exciting design concept. The issue of repetition, inherent in mass-production systems, led to other interesting design explorations. The relationship between identical units was explored through the geometry of transformation, translation, rotation and reflection, together with the notions of stacking, nesting and fitting[6]. The issue of linear repetition was considered as something which would modify the historical idea of rhythm in architecture[7].

The third issue was the concept of 'elementalism'. Prior to the twentieth century, reference to 'elements' in architecture would have been a reference to the Platonic volumes of a design and how they could be brought together in a satisfactory composition according to the rules identified by such Beaux-Arts theorists as Charles Blanc in his *Grammaire des Arts de Dessin* of 1867 or Julien Guadet in *Eléments et Théories de L'Architecture*. Through the discourse of the Bauhaus in Germany, the De Stijl group in Holland and the Constructivists in Russia, the meaning of the word changed to apply to the individual structural parts of a building, and in particular to the visual separation of these into identifiable elements. An examination of this change will help to identify the meaning and significance of the new use of the word 'element'. Two closely interwoven issues come together: a sense of visual abstraction from the De Stijl, movement and an expressive use of structure from the Constructivists.

Reyner Banham in *Theory and Design in the First Machine Age* refers to the rationalist influences of the De Stijl group architect and theorist Hendrikus Peter Berlage[8]:

> Rationalist and disciplined, exclusive not inclusive, preferring a limited range of materials, forms and structural methods.

The De Stijl use of visual abstraction is particularly explicit when Berlage writes in *Grundlagen und Entwicklung der Architektur* of 1908:

> Before all else the wall must be shown naked in all its sleek beauty, and anything fixed on to it must be shunned as an embarrassment. . . . And thus walling would receive its due value again, in the sense that its nature as a plane would remain.

This abstraction, this separate visual reading of each wall and floor plane, is clearly identifiable at the Schroeder House of 1925 at Utrecht by Gerrit Thomas Rietveld (Figure 9.1), and similarly in the visual separation of each of the constructional parts of his chair of 1917 (Figure 9.2). It is in this mental separation of each part of the construction which makes each part into an abstract, non-representational 'element'.

Figure 9.1 Schroder House, 1925; Gerrit Thomas Rietveld (courtesy of the Architectural Press photographic library)

Figure 9.2 Rietveld chair, 1917; Gerrit Thomas Rietveld (courtesy of the Architectural Press photographic library)

The Constructivists made use of the abstract and non-representational qualities of the separate elements of a building as a means to break from the past. They used the separate elements of structure as an emotive expression of a new industrialized socialist society. These ideals were for the most part expressed only in words and images, but a few projects did get built. The Makhorka Pavilion by K. S. Melnikov (Figure 9.3) and the Izvestia Pavilion by Exter and Gladhov (Figure 9.4), both for the Agriculture Exhibition at Moscow in 1923, demonstrate construction expressed as separate elements. The construction is used overtly, uncompromised and unhidden. The separate and visually identifiable constructional parts are attached but

Figure 9.3 Makhorka Pavilion, Agricultural Exhibition, Moscow, 1923; K. S. Melnikov (reproduced from *Style and Epoch*, Moisei Ginzburg, courtesy of MIT Press)

Figure 9.4 Izvestia Pavilion, Agricultural Exhibition, Moscow, 1923; Exter and Gladkov (reproduced from *Style and Epoch*, Moisei Ginzburg, courtesy of MIT Press)

never intermoulded. The apparent separation of the parts gives a sense of daring structural balance. This new types of visual syntax is particularly apparent in Alexander Vesnin's stage set for 'The Man Who Was Thursday' (Figure 9.5). Here the elemental form of construction is particularly expressive of industry and the machine.

All of this engenders Ginzburg's feeling for the 'pulse and rhythm of industry in society' which he describes in the chapter 'The Prerequisites of the New Style' in *Stil'i Epokha* [9]:

> The deafening roar of orderly monster-machines; the rhythmic operation of pulleys, uniting everything and everyone with their movement; the rays of light penetrating the taut veil of glass and steel; and the collective output of valuable products extruded from the creative crucible. Can there be a picture that more clearly reflects the purposeful way of life of modernity?

Figure 9.5 Stage set for 'The Man Who Was Thursday', 1923; A. A. Vesnin (reproduced from *Style and Epoch*, Moisei Ginzburg, courtesy of MIT Press)

This is powerfully expressed in Vladimir Tatlin's use of construction as a statement of Socialist ideals in his project, designed in 1919–20, for the 303 metre high Monument to the Third International (Figure 9.6).

Construction became central to the expression of art and architecture. The genesis of this is traceable to such works of art as Vladimir Tatlin's experimental 'counter-reliefs', constructed in 1913–14, which emphasized the 'use of real materials in real space'. Fundamental to these beliefs was the conceptual shift from the flat canvas of painting to the more 'constructive' medium of the three-dimensional object, reflecting not only the intrinsic nature of the materials employed but also the means of combining and supporting them. [10].

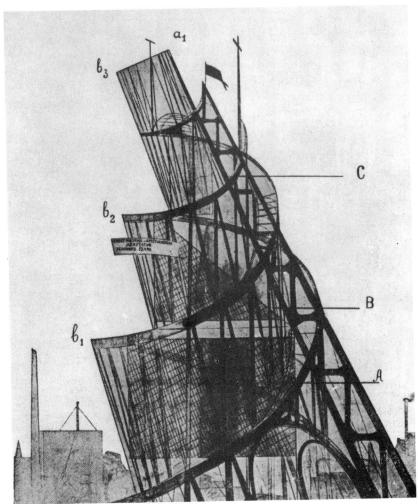

Figure 9.6 Monument to the Third International, 1919–20; Vladimir Tatlin

This idea was extended by the work of the architect–artist El Lissitzky, whose interest in the visual power of construction and the need to break out from the restrictions of the painters canvas led to his three-dimensional abstract art forms entitled 'Prouns', a name derived from an abbreviation of Russian words meaning 'project for the establishment of a new art'. Lissitzky recorded his thoughts in his paper *Proun: Not World Vision But World Reality* of 1920:

> The artist is turning from an imitator into a constructor of new world objects.

Architecture and art came together in his 'Proun Room' for the Berlin Art Exhibition of 1923 (Figure 9.7).

One of the most successful designers to turn these ideas into architectural reality was the French industrialist Jean Prouvé. His work stands as an example of the new type of art which could be generated from the practical use of the new materials and the new processing machines and techniques. Prouvé's particular interest was in the machine working of metals, its implications on industrialized construction, and its influence on the design and appearance of objects. He set up a workshop at Nancy in 1923 where he experimented with electric welding and the use of folded metal sheets. This innovative work led him to work with the architects Mallet-Stevens and P. Herbe. He moved to larger premises in 1931 and set up the prefabrication company Ateliers Jean Prouvé. During the 1930s he developed his ideas. His credo was to bring the building process within the influence of the industrial miracle of the machine[11].

He developed his metal structures and claddings through a series of commissions and prototype systems. In 1931 he won a competition with a system of movable metal internal walls. In 1935 he worked in

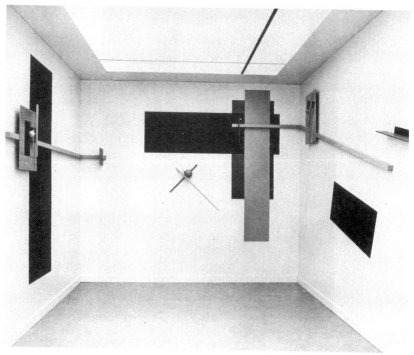

Figure 9.7 Proun Room exhibit, 1923; El Lissitzky

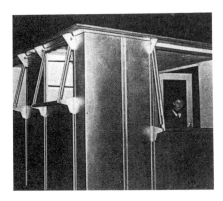

Figure 9.8 BLPS lightweight metal houses, 1935; Prouvé, Beaudoin and Lods (reproduced from *Jean Prouvé*, Huber and Steinegger)

Figure 9.9 Maison du Peuple de Clichy, 1938–9, Prouvé, Beaudoin, Lods and Bodiansky (reproduced from *Jean Prouvé*, Huber and Steinegger)

collaboration with the architects Beaudoin and Lods for the design of the BLPS system of prefabricated lightweight houses (Figure 9.8). He recognized that the new methods of steel construction gave the buildings a distinct architectural character of their own; they were light and dynamic, the true characteristics of large-scale industrial production.

His working with Beaudoin and Lods led him in 1936 into collaboration with the engineer Vladimir Bodiansky, who was then working with Eugène Mopin. Collectively they designed and built the Maison du Peuple de Clichy in 1938–9 (Figure 9.9). This covered market demonstrates the amount of research and experimentation which Prouvé realized to be necessary to produce the new architecture. However, World War II halted Prouvé's plans to set up larger production runs.

10 The building component as an element in design, 1945–1970

This chapter considers how industrialization of the building industry since World War II has led to an increase in the availability of inter-usable standardized building components. It considers the significance which this increase in the use of components has had on architectural design.

During the inter-war period, the development of industrialized building systems was seen as a way of solving the shortage of buildings. The growth of prototypes for new systems was encouraged by the acute need for houses and also by the designers who associated the new industrialized images with modern design. In spite of these stimulants, the sheer size of projects needed to make each system practical, together with the enormous finance required, proved too much for the intransigent opinions of the government administrators. Although a few systems did make a start in the mid-1930s, the administrative hurdles were never completely overcome before World War II put an abrupt stop to the development of system building.

Although the war caused a six-year halt in the development of system building, paradoxically it also provided, through the need to replace the great number of buildings lost during the war, the necessary additional stimulant to set system building off on a more urgent and enthusiastic start after the war.

A review of the building industry's response to the post-war challenge reveals the evolution of certain significant developments, which gradually affected the common practice of assembling buildings and, through this, influenced the way in which designers considered the nature and morphology of buildings. A central issue was the progressive dependence upon the building component as both a convenient and an aesthetic unit of construction. An examination of the development of system building from 1945 to the mid-1960s reveals a slow move from the early 'closed' systems of the 1940s, which used their own 'taylor-made' kit of parts, to the more 'open' systems of the 1960s, which were able to make use of common building units which were interchangeable between the various systems. These interchangeable units eventually became the components of an internationally available kit of parts from which designers could freely choose. This chapter reveals how the movement away from 'closed' systems to the 'open' use of components gradually modified the architectural grammar of buildings.

Housing was immediately given priority in Britain at the end of World War II. The Government Command Paper of March 1945, *Housing* (Command 6609), stated that the first objective was to provide a separate dwelling for every family that wanted one. It estimated that this would need about three-quarters of a million new houses. The second objective was to complete the slum clearance programmes initiated before the war[1].

The gravity of the situation led the government to recognize the necessity for mass orders to realize the economic advantages of system construction. The government's first initiative was to build mass, cheap and temporary houses to overcome the immediate emergency. The Housing (Temporary Accommodation) Act of October 1944 authorized the construction of 400 000 houses, each with an intended life span of ten years and an estimated cost of £375. This ambitious Act had been based on prototypes carried out for the prefabricated 'Portal House', named after Lord Portal, then Minister of Works. The programme, however, soon came face to face with the reality of running an enormous mass-production 'closed' system. The Portal House had been designed around the use of pressed steel and plywood, which on investigation were found to be unobtainable in sufficient quantities to run the production line. The government had to change course to achieve the number of temporary houses required, and adopted eleven different designs for mass production. The main contributors were the Aluminium Bungalow, the Arcon prefabricated house and the Uni-Seco prefabricated house. This subdivision of the programme was better suited to the actual situation at the end of the war. It spread demand over a larger number of the restricted materials, and each manufacturer was able to make separate use of the redundant munitions assembly line factories scattered around the country. The numbers of prefabs actually completed were: Aluminium Bungalows 55 000, Arcon 41 000 and Uni-Seco 29 000. The final costs eventually averaged out at £1300 per dwelling[2]. These figures were scorned in Parliament and swung opinion away from prefabricated system building. This was regrettable as it denied recognition of the results produced so quickly by the manufacturers, rather than questioning the unrealistic dreams which the originators in government had had about mass-production.

The achievements in terms of an advancement in prefabricated construction is illustrated by the Aluminium Bungalow project. This was the most highly prefabricated house in the programme. It was mass-produced on an assembly line (Figure 10.1) using aluminium wall trays filled with air-entrained grout formed into units larger than ever previously envisaged (Figure 10.2). Each dwelling thus consisted of only four transportable parts. The units were designed around the maximum permitted road transport width of 2.3 metres; its heaviest unit, which contained the back-to-back kitchen and bathroom, was designed down to the maximum lorry load of 16 tonnes. The units were jointed on site using spring-clipped aluminium cover-strips (Figure 10.3). The project was also innovative in its structural use of aluminium for building. The structural use of aluminium dates from 1909 when the German Alfred Wilm discovered the age-hardening

Figure 10.1 Assembly line for the Aluminium Bungalow, 1945 (reproduced from *Prefabrication*, R. B. White, with permission of the Controller of Her Majesty's Stationery Office)

Figure 10.2 Prefabricated units for the Aluminium Bungalow, 1945 (reproduced from *Prefabrication*, R. B. White, courtesy of the Aluminium Federation)

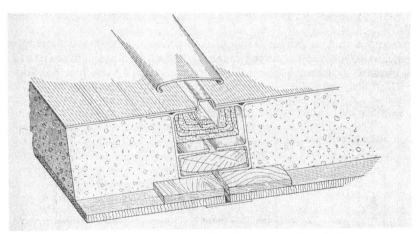

Figure 10.3 Site jointing detail for the Aluminium Bungalow, 1945 (reproduced from *Prefabrication*, R. B. White, courtesy of the Aluminium Federation)

alloy which led to Duralumin, produced by Durenner Metalwerke and used extensively for the Zeppelins in World War I[3,4]. The Aluminium Bungalow prefab project made use of the aircraft production lines released at the end of the war and was designed to utilize the surplus and scrap aluminium alloy then available. Much of the interior structure was made using lightweight aluminium alloy.

The optimism with which the Temporary Housing Programme was set up continued to drive system building forward during the 1950s. The political and social need for new buildings, and the excitement of the new form of architecture involved, kept the utopian dream alive. There was a sense of optimism about system building, an optimism which looked attractive in theory but, as proved by the Temporary Housing Programme, would not hold up to its theoretical potential when run in practice. There were too many building firms seeking the limited resources of government and, in spite of the government's attempt to make accurate statistical comparisons between the contenders, the systems were never reduced to a realistic number to allow sufficiently large orders to be placed to make them viable. Local authorities continued to see their housing programme in terms of small, scattered pockets of land with one system used for one site and another system for another. Seldom could an economic run of a particular type of house be counted on in any one place over a number of years.

The systems which did manage to attract an economic production run all survived by pursuing a competitive and practical reality.

One system which survived the economic restraints was the Airey House (Figure 10.4). These were formed using 100 × 65 mm precast concrete posts at 450 mm centres to the front and rear elevations,

Figure 10.4 Airey Rural House Type, 1945 (reproduced from *Prefabrication*, R. B. White, with permission of the Controller of Her Majesty's Stationery Office)

connected across by lightweight steel lattice joists. The precast concrete cladding panels were 900 mm long and 250 mm high. All the parts which made up the system were small enough to be man-handled to allow the house to be constructed on the scattered, often remote or rural sites around the country[5]. This design restraint of small units gave the cladding panels a domestic, small-scale appearance suitable for rural areas, but it is a pity that this ruralism led Sir Edwin Airey away from industrialized design solutions in favour of traditional tiled roofs and brick outbuildings.

One system which managed to break out of the traditional house image, and yet remain financially viable, was the Reema System. The sponsors and designers, Messrs Reed and Malik of Salisbury, right from the beginning in 1945 chose to use derricks and cranes to permit the movement of large, storey-height, double-skin, precast concrete panels (Figure 10.5). The early dwellings were two-storey with a traditional timber and tile roof, but by the late 1950s they had improved the system to build modern-looking blocks of flats of up to ten storeys. Mr Reed was determined to produce cheap but well-built mass-produced homes and was prepared to let the pragmatic factors of construction influence the appearance of the buildings.

One problem which arose from the use of large panels was that they tended to collect and accentuate any differential movement at the

Figure 10.5 Precast concrete panels for the Reema House, 1945 (reproduced from *Prefabrication*, R. B. White, courtesy of Reema Construction)

joints between the panels. It is interesting to note that the Reema System developed an open-recessed, drained and flashed joint between the panels, in place of the previously used filled and cover strip joint (Figure 10.6).

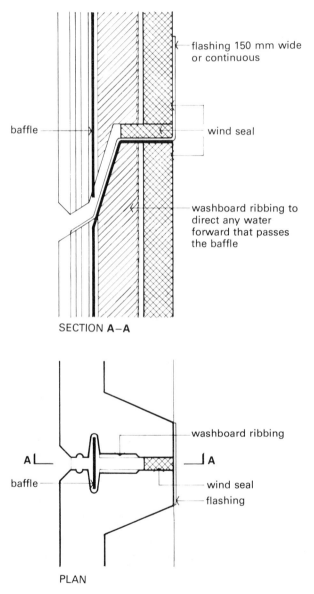

Figure 10.6 Open-drained joint for precast concrete panels (reproduced from *Precast Concrete Cladding*, W. R. Oram, courtesy of the British Cement Association)

The problem of movement between panels had previously been investigated by the Building Research Station in 1947, where they carried out tests in collaboration with the railways to overcome the problem of vibration from passing trains. The prototype building of 1948 at Queen's Park Station (Figure 10.7) represents an early use of flexible mastic joints between the panels. The panels were also experimental, being an early use of preformed vitreous-enamelled steel trays [6].

The process of prefabrication and the use of components was further encouraged by the development, during the early 1950s, of flexible mastics. This was encouraged by the introduction of neoprene into building construction. An article in *Architectural Forum*, November 1954, 'The General Motors Technical Centre', describes Eero Saarinen's innovative detailing:

> Industrial components of the curtain wall – double glazing and porcelain enamel panels . . . are gripped like automobile windshields to their metal frames with extruded neoprene gaskets . . . set in place on the lips of the aluminium sections, the glass or porcelain enamel panel is slid into place, then the joints are 'zipped' tight by inserting the filler strip of neoprene.

This represents one of the earliest modern curtain walls. The office

Figure 10.7 Queen's Park Station, London, 1948 (reproduced from *Prefabrication*, R. B. White, with permission of the Controller of Her Majesty's Stationery Office)

block in New Cavendish Street, London 1955–7, by Gollins Melvin and Ward (Figure 10.8) generated a lot of interest and praise for the stark simplicity of its curtain-wall facades.

One of the more financially minded of the building companies was Wates Ltd. They carefully developed their load-bearing precast concrete panel system from their house type of the late 1940s (Figures 10.9 and 10.10) through the 1950s to a system in the early 1960s which could stack up to six storeys. However, even Wates' order book was insufficient for them to produce a pure mass-produced system. In their later houses the prefabricated inner linings of the walls were abandoned in favour of lightweight concrete blocks which were then plastered, and the light prefabricated roof sections were replaced by conventional timber rafters.

The British government did not have the political desire, nor the platform, to force through dictatorial measures to set up large mass-production runs to construct block after block of identical dwelling units.

Although the political will did not exist in Britain, the central authority of some governments of eastern Europe did encourage and set up large mass-production runs. It is in these large repetitive projects that the architectural grammar of the closed prefabricated system is most clearly expressed. The mass-housing development in East Berlin (Figure 10.11) serves as a typical example.

Figure 10.8 Curtain wall glazing, 93–97 New Cavendish Street, London, 1955–7; Gollins Melvin and Ward (photograph James Strike)

Figure 10.9 Erection of precast concrete units, Wates System, 1940s (reproduced from *Prefabrication*, R. B. White, courtesy of Wates Construction Ltd)

Figure 10.10 Precast, tray-shaped, concrete panels, Wates System, 1940s (reproduced from *Prefabrication*, R. B. White, courtesy of Wates Construction Ltd)

Figure 10.11 Mass Housing, East Berlin (photograph James Strike)

Alternative arrangements had to be found in Britain to set up markets and orders of sufficient size to retain the economic advantages of industrial production. Two events helped towards solving this problem: the setting up of dimensional coordinates for the building industry and the grouping of similar building programmes into consortia.

It was realized that there were advantages to be gained from building components which could be used in more than one of the numerous building systems. It was also recognized that the key to such arrangements would be the coordination of the size of the components. Research was carried out between 1951 and 1955 by Rodney Thomas on behalf of the Arcon Group to devise a set of 'variable adaptors' which would adjust the size of existing components to make them up to a standardized coordinated component (Figure 10.12)[7]. However, these were not popular as they were contrary to the financial and aesthetic qualities of 'directness and simplicity' which designers were looking for in prefabrication. The Modular Society was founded in 1953 to promote the adoption of preferred dimensions throughout the building industry. It envisaged modular coordinated dimensions controlling the industry, from the smallest component to the height of a storey and the width of a bay. It had considerable success with new systems and new commodities such as alloy windows[8] and synthetic composite boards[9], but in general did not achieve the expected overall change to existing systems and long-established materials such as bricks and doors, which were so rooted in imperial measurements. Standardization did, however, move the manufacturers towards cost savings, higher performance and greater precision.

A   basic pieces
B   structural tolerance take up piece
C   edge conversion piece
D   make up piece

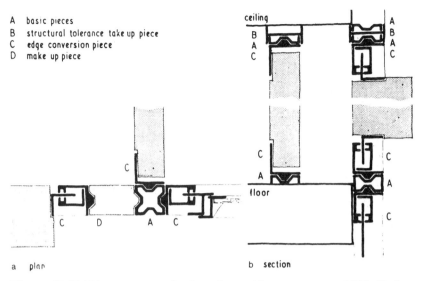

a   plan

b   section

Figure 10.12 Edge converter for interchangeable components, 1955; Rodney Thomas (reproduced from *Architectural Review*, September 1955)

Discussions took place between designers and manufacturers so that the contractors could turn towards 'fit', 'clarity of construction' and a sense of three-dimensional 'purity'. This belief in a mathematical order has occurred throughout architectural history as a controlling device. It now invaded beyond the plan and section to control and influence the construction of buildings. The alignment of the components, and the clarity of the joints between them, gave the architecture a hard-edged clarity[10]. This is seen in the Charles Eames House (Figure 10.13), where the selected components stack up between the black lines of the jointing system to form a large Mondrian painting[11].

Consortia were set up so that similar building programmes could be grouped together into large rolling programmes of sufficient size to benefit from bulk purchasing and serial tendering. They would also benefit from collaborative research and shared development costs. The pioneer of this approach was the Consortium of Local Authorities Special Programme (CLASP), which was first set up in 1957 through the joining together of the building programmes of Derbyshire, Durham, Glamorgan, West Riding of Yorkshire and Nottinghamshire County Councils and the Coventry and Leicester City Councils. The initiative came from the Nottinghamshire County Council which, having built new schools using their own standardized prefabricated

Figure 10.13 The Eames House, 1947; Charles Eames (reproduced courtesy of Architectural Design, London)

system, saw the economic advantage of ordering large quantities of standardized building units. The Nottinghamshire form of construction, designed by Donald Gibson, then County Architect, was based on the experience gained by the Hertfordshire County Council, which had developed their system for building schools since 1946 using a prefabricated lightweight metal frame with prefabricated cladding panels. The Ministry of Education Building Bulletin No.19, *The Story of CLASP*, refers to the first of these Hertfordshire schools at Cheshunt:

> . . . in many ways one of the most important post-war British buildings. Certainly, its influence on the subsequent development of other systems of prefabricated school construction has been profound.

Donald Gibson capitalized on this early experience and made use of the experimental steel-frame construction which had been developed by the Ministry of Education for the pilot project of 1953–4 for the Secondary Modern School at Belper, Derbyshire. He thus achieved a means of constructing lightweight and flexible structures which would overcome the problem of building on subsidence-prone ground over the coal mining areas of Nottinghamshire. It was this form of construction which was adopted by the CLASP consortium (Figure 10.14).

The CLASP team set out on what was to become a full and successful programme of construction. The number of schools submitted for the programme in 1958–9 was 31. By 1965 the number of projects had risen to 124 from a membership of 16 authorities, with 14 other associate members[12]. Throughout this period there had

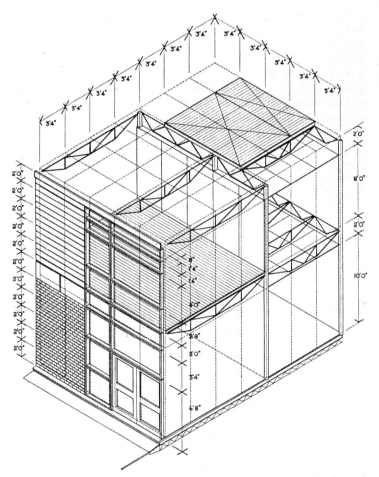

Figure 10.14 CLASP Construction, 1960: isometric projection of a typical building showing the relationship between the various components and the module lines, both vertical and horizontal (reproduced from *CLASP Construction 1960*, with permission of the Controller of Her Majesty's Stationery Office)

been a vigorous process of feedback, reappraisal, adjustment and fine tuning of the details, all of which helped to make the system both competitive and desirable. Its success was also encouraged by the building of a CLASP school at the 1960 Triennale di Milano where it was awarded the Special Grand Prize.

Several issues arose out of the CLASP building programme which were to modify the way in which buildings were assembled. During the gradual process of improving the system, there had been an increase in the dialogue between the designers and the manufacturers. This dialogue, about standardization of dimensions and the process and problems of assembly, together with the increased size of orders made possible by consortia programmes, led the manufacturers to a commitment to the concept of the prefabricated building component. This stronger financial situation, together with the increased number of units produced, and the improvement in the dimensional coordination of the components, all helped to move the consortium buildings from 'closed' constructional systems towards more 'open' and inter-usable methods of assembly.

By the mid-1960s, the manufacturers had begun to build up a stock of interchangeable building components, for example Beclawat aluminium windows, Metsec steel trusses, standardized door units, etc. These components were not locked into a particular closed system of construction, but freely available for all designers to use.

The increased stock of available and interchangeable building units made it possible for designers, even those using a system such as CLASP, to have more flexibility to respond to the specific need of each project; cladding panels could be selected to suit regional character-istics, and fixtures and finishes selected to suit the particular requirements of each client. For the individual designer, not locked into a particular system of construction, the range of building components coming onto the market provided new opportunities. It gave designers an extended selection of items with which to build, no longer restricted to traditional materials, but able to explore industrialized images used in what could be referred to as a 'free form' system of prefabrication.

Cedric Price pursued this idea of a flexible assemblage of standard components in the early 1960s. His approach led to an architecture which grew naturally out of a free assembly of standard components to form the client's required enclosure, the idea being that such construction would liberate the client from conventional architectural values[13]. He explored this notion through some concept drawings such as his futuristic mega-structure for Joan Littlewood's Fun Palace. However, it was not until 1977 that he realized this philosophy through the building of the Interaction Centre at Kentish Town (Figure 10.15). Here he used 'off the peg' prefabricated building components freely assembled in a direct response to the user's requirements.

Another factor which arose from the growth in the use of building components, and which simultaneously led to a change of design values, was the emergence of a new method of jointing. Over the years the method of jointing had gradually progressed from a closed, filled or covered joint to a new type of open, recessed and drained joint; this led to a new type of architectural language. For example, comparison between the coverstrip jointing over the prefabricated cladding of the Kleinhaus experimental house by Gropius in 1927 (Figure 8.10) and the uncovered joint between the vitreous-enamelled panels used for Queen's Park Railway Station in 1948 (Figure 10.7) demonstrates the change. The recess, formed by the open joint, at Queen's Park station helps to accentuate the visually separate and individual statement of each unit of construction, compared with the earlier covered joint at Kleinhaus where a 'ladder-rack' lattice work, formed by the

Figure 10.15 The Interaction Community Centre, Kentish Town, London, 1977; Cedric Price (courtesy of the Architectural Press photographic library)

Figure 10.16 Elgin Estate, Paddington, London, 1968; Greater London Council (photograph James Strike)

cover-strips, visually reduces the units of construction to the status of a subordinate infill panel. This change from a cohesive lattice frame with infill panels to a piling up of visually separate blocks (similar to children's building bricks) slowly matured, and the new expression is clearly seen at the Elgin Estates, Paddington, built by the GLC in 1968 (Figure 10.16). The factory-made panels are shaped to stand proud of the dark recess of the gasket joint.

These panels are an early use of glass reinforced plastic, they incorporate standard bus-type window components, and their soft curvature reflects the manufacturing process. Their size and visual separation give the building a new sense of scale. The panels read as separate digits; each panel reads as a separate constructional element and, in doing so, provides a new category of design grammar, far removed from the monolithic appearance of *in-situ* concrete or the fine-grained texture of a brickwork building.

11 1970–1990, an appraisal

This book began by identifying an hypothesis which proposed that the introduction of new building materials and new forms of construction have, over a period of time, led to a change in architectural design. It then used a series of historical episodes to trace this idea since the Industrial Revolution. This final chapter acts as an appraisal of these separate studies; it aims to establish some form of criticism of the role of construction in contemporary architectural design, and looks for underlying principles and significant recurring trends which would shed light on, and help us in evaluating, the present situation. The intention is not to prove or disprove the hypothesis, nor even to arrive at some calculated quotient between right and wrong, but to seek a clearer and wider understanding of the issues.

It is evident from the historical studies that the subject is complex. The topics interconnect within a wide range of related issues, as diverse and as powerful as social concern, finance, politics, war and fashion.

Although it is apparent from the historical studies that new materials and new constructional techniques have brought about a change in architectural design, it is equally apparent that new materials and forms of construction have arisen in response to the forces of architectural fashion and social concern. The relationship between these two routes is interwoven and complex. It is, to take an example, difficult to differentiate between the twin stimuli which led to the use of prefabricated components to build the postwar primary schools; there was, on one hand, the external influence of the economic thrust from social concern and the need for a school place for every child, and, on the other, the aspiration to use the new forms of industrialized construction to create modern design.

The separate historical studies, by the nature of the specific route of the examination, are determinist in the story depicted for each particular material or technique. Each has been edited to relate to the study, and as such is unable to encompass the full cross-grained reality of historical events. It would therefore be impossible to attempt to establish some definite conclusion. The aim, therefore, is to approach the examination in a somewhat philosophical manner, and, in doing so, to hold on to the phrase 'towards a broader vision' used by Bertrand Russell to explain Plato's persistent interrogation of his contemporaries about their ideas on absolute truth[1].

The appraisal follows several lines of thought. First, it considers *the changing viewpoint*. This reviews the constant shift of opinion by which designers, and society in general, have viewed the use of new technology in the creation of contemporary architecture. It is through this shift of opinion that the evolution of constructional methods has had to pass. Second, it examines *the nature of change*. This identifies recurring characteristics within the process by which new materials and new forms of construction progress from the tentative early experiments to become a recognized part of common architectural practice. Third, it looks for long-term developments in the evolution of materials or types of construction which can be recognized as common *evolutionary themes*.

The changing viewpoint

An appraisal of the historical studies will not be easy. It is evident that there are no clearcut growth patterns, no straightforward sequences. One reason for this is the frequent change in the way in which different groups have viewed the role of technology in the design process. This has occurred not only in the form of one generation reacting against its predecessor, but also as opposing points of view at any given period. It is through this shift of opinion that the development of constructional techniques has had to evolve.

This oscillation created an uncertain climate for the growth of technological development. There have therefore been no straightline graphs of evolution; in fact the graphs have often wobbled so much that their long-term direction has sometimes seemed in doubt.

These long-term changes will be considered under the heading of *evolutionary themes*, but first it is necessary to look at the way in which the perception of technology has changed through history.

It is apparent from the historical studies that the Industrial Revolution brought to the second half of the eighteenth century a divided opinion. There were the owners of the new mills and iron foundries who had an enthusiastic and thrusting attitude towards innovation and technology, and there were those who thought that these changes represented the end of everything wholesome. The debate raged between industry and nature[2], between the beauty of the rustic and picturesque and the power of working machinery and a productive economy.

This conflict continued throughout the nineteenth century, but there grew, during the latter part of the century, an opinion which recognized beauty within the innovations. This beauty lay in an honest, direct and non-historical use of modern methods of construction.

The shock of World War I had a swift effect on opinions and values so that there was, by the close of the war, a need and an enthusiasm for scientific methodology. Although there was a lot of debate and preparation of reports during the inter-war period, little was done to set up new industrialized production. There was a strong desire to hold onto the pre-war style of life.

The struggle of World War II stimulated innovation and new technology, and the destruction caused by the war created the need and willingness to pursue industrialization of building. This interest in a functional and industrial approach gradually influenced architectural thinking. A great deal of design work was carried out within scientifically motivated research and development groups. Design became a corporate rather than an individual activity.

During the mid-1960s doubts began to be raised concerning the general consensus that design should stem from purely rational analysis. It is interesting to note, however, that the validity of a functional approach to design had been questioned years earlier; the American architect Joseph Hudnut, in *The Post Modern House* of 1945, referred to the need for a house to be more than a machine, it also needed to express 'the idea of home'. This new mood, for an architecture able to symbolize emotional and historical values, was publicized through Robert Venturi's influential book *Complexity and Contradiction in Architecture* of 1966; the notion was pursued, in terms of technology, by Alan Colquhoun, who, in *Symbolic and Literal Aspects of Technology* of 1962, explored the idea that the construction detailing used by the architects of the Modern Movement had been designed to be modern, not only in a scientific and technical sense, but also to express modernity as an artistic symbolism for the new age[3]:

> Our admiration of the buildings it created is due more to their success as symbolic representations than to the extent to which they solved technical problems.

By the 1970s design had gradually moved away from scientific advancement to become more a symbolic working of the visual ingredients of the Modern Movement. Symbolism was used to create a stylishly modern building; modern forms of construction were used, not to produce solutions to modern problems, but as an expedient reason for producing stylish buildings within the economic restraints. Walter Gropius was thus proved correct in his prediction that there would be 'imitations which distorted the fundamental truth'[4]. It is the constructional failure of these superficial copies which has given the Modern Movement such a bad press.

Reaction against these latterday Modern Movement buildings helped to strengthen the swing of opinion away from technologically based architecture, so that by the 1980s most new buildings had an historical appearance. This took two forms; there were the 'neo-vernacular' housing estates and shopping centres, and later in the 1980s 'post-modern' office blocks and designer studios. It is interesting to observe that both these architectural styles used modern methods of construction. The 'neo-vernacular' houses used prefabricated structural panels, usually timber, covered with country brickwork. The shopping centres, meant to resemble agricultural barns, were built with large-span steel frames and small areas of tiled roofs. Modern forms of gaskets and anti-corrosive fixings enabled the 'post-modern' designers to hang their historical symbols, pediments and capitals, on to hidden structures as visually separate motifs.

Although historical style took precedence over technologically motivated architecture during the 1980s, there had always existed a lifeline of interest in the expression of construction. This had its origins in the science and the images of modern technology. it expressed the constructional systems implicit in the silicon chip and space exploration. This expressionist use of technology had in fact occurred in earlier buildings such as the Crystal House of 1933 by William and George Keck (Figure 11.1). The interest in the techniques and images of space exploration was pursued during the 1960s by the speculative projects of Peter Cook and Ron Herron. Their schemes were futuristic megastructures, city-sized machines reminiscent of the film sets for *Metropolis* and *Things to Come*[5].

It was not until the mid-1970s that the constructional reasoning of technologically based design was used in live projects. One of the most influential buildings was the Centre National d'Art et de Culture Georges Pompidou by Renzo Piano and Richard Rogers of 1971–7 (Figure 11.2). Many buildings followed this approach, albeit often

Figure 11.1 The Crystal House, 1933; William and George Keck (reproduced from *American Architecture*, David Handlin

with more interest in the image of technology rather than its use to fulfil a specific need. Peter Rice, the structural engineer for the Pompidou Centre, describes these buildings which became tagged 'high-tech' as 'a misunderstanding of the role of technology in the image of a building'[6]. There were, however, architects who pursued a more rigorous approach towards the natural expression of construction to solve specific requirements. Jan Kaplicky and David Nixon, for example, pursued this through their Future Systems projects such as the Nursery Shed of 1984 (Figure 11.3).

The use of modern technology gradually became more confident. Human requirements for comfort have become greater decade by decade, and the facilities required by business and industry continue to increase with the development of new systems. Designers now use construction in a more thoughtful and less stylistic way to fulfil these new expectations. Carefully detailed and assembled constructions are being calculated as a natural and direct response to the client's needs. The work of Renzo Piano demonstrates this tendency. The Menil Arts Gallery, Houston, 1981–3 (Figure 11.4) is a building sensitively edited and executed to control the harsh Texan sunlight. The aesthetic and scientific study of the light generated the large ferro-cement leaves to provide natural light for the works of art (Figure 11.5). Similarly,

Figure 11.2 Centre National d'Art et de Culture Georges Pompidou, Les Halles, Beaubourg, Paris, 1971–7; Renzo Piano and Richard Rogers (photograph Bastiaan Valkenburg)

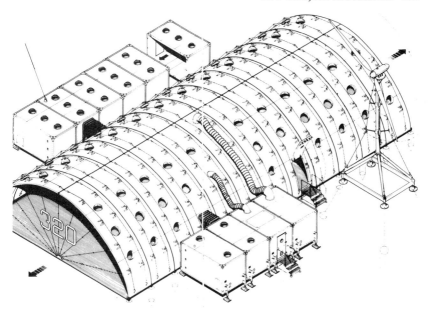

Figure 11.3 Nursery Shed Project, 1984; Jan Kaplicky and David Nixon

Figure 11.4 Menil Arts Gallery, Houston, Texas, 1981–3; Renzo Piano

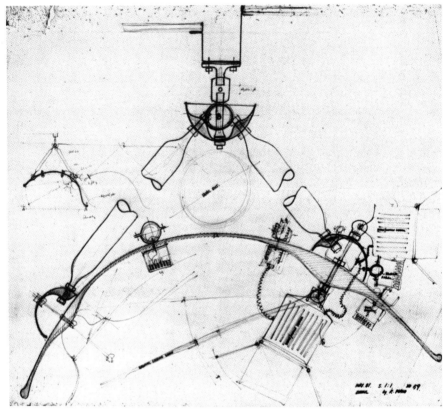

Figure 11.5 Detail of roof light filter leaf, Menil Arts Gallery, Houston, Texas, 1981–3; Renzo Piano (reproduced from *Renzo Piano*, Massimo Dini

there is a relaxed economy in Glen Murcutt's use of simple materials to construct the Bingie Bingie house at Mount Irvine, Australia, 1988 (Figure 11.6). Here again its assembly grows out of climate and location. There is a sense of an architecture which is responding to regional differences, not based on materials, as were the buildings of the pre-industrial age, but on climate. The structure and detailing of these buildings is quieter than the earlier 'high-tech' buildings. Their architectural strength is a thoughtful economy and a scientific response to human need. Richard Horden's lecture at the Royal Institute of British Architects in 1989[7], 'The Thinking Glass Skin', highlighted how new technologies can be used to solve the ever-increasing demands of environmental control. Modern science has made it possible for the skin of a building to monitor and adapt to climatic

End view

Living room

Figure 11.6 The Bingie Bingie House at Mount Irvine, Australia, 1988; Glenn Murcutt (courtesy of Glen Murcutt)

change to maintain a balanced and pleasant internal environment. His office block at Stag Place, Victoria, London, 1989, illustrates the evolving architecture through the double layer of 'thinking' glass skin which forms the elevation (Figure 11.7).

The nature of change

It is evident from the historical studies that new materials and constructional techniques often took a considerable period of time to

Figure 11.7 Office Block, Stag Place, Victoria, London, 1988; Richard Horden (reproduced from *Architectural Review*, January 1988)

be absorbed into architectural design. This slowness is a recurring theme. For example, cast iron, smelted by Abraham Darby in 1709, did not become a common commodity in building construction until the 1790s. Similarly, Portland cement, patented by Joseph Aspdin in 1794, was not used extensively until the beginning of the twentieth century. And aluminium, invented in 1807, commercially produced in 1890, was not used extensively in the building trade until 1945. These instances reveal that, although the construction industry has changed fundamentally during the last two hundred years, the changes did not take place quickly or willingly. There is a sense of reluctance to accept innovation. Rudyard Kipling, writing in the 1890s, encapsulates the conservative nature of the building industry[8]:

> I tell this tale, which is strictly true,
> Just by way of convincing you
> How very little, since things were made,
> Things have changed in the building trade.

There were, of course, much stronger voices of criticism such as Ruskin, who in the 1850s wrote vehemently against the new form of iron construction[9]:

> Perhaps the most fruitful source of corruption which we have had to guard against in recent times is . . . the use of iron . . . The Art of Architecture is independent of materials.

Machiavelli wrote in even more fundamental terms about the reluctance to change[10]:

> There is nothing more difficult to carry out, nor more doubtful of success, nor more dangerous to handle, than to initiate a new order of things. For the reformer has enemies in all who profit by the old order, and only lukewarm defenders in all those who would profit by the new order. This lukewarmness arises . . . from the incredulity of mankind who do not truly believe in anything new until they have had actual experience of it.

The historical studies show, however, that the new ideas did eventually come to be used in architectural construction. They also indicate that the long path towards acceptance frequently followed a recurring pattern. The story line for each material or technique is never identical, but the recurring stages often include: inception of the idea, testing of prototypes, trial use, failure, gestation on the shelf, reinvention, retrial, success through the construction of a seminal building, adoption, misuse, rejection due to failure or a change of fashion, introduction of legislation to control its use, gradual improvement of the material or technique, and finally general acceptance.

A closer look at these stages helps to broaden our understanding of the process.

The moment of origin of an idea is often unclear. Similar exploratory work often took place at the same time and the authorship and date of many inventions was disputed. The historical studies do reveal, however, several recurring sources for the inception of new building materials and new types of construction. One of the most frequent sources was an attempt to find a cheaper, more readily available or easier to produce substitute for an existing material. This is clearly seen in the experiments carried out by Joseph Aspdin in 1794 which culminated in his patent of 1824 for Portland Cement: his intention was to manufacture an economic rendering to imitate Portland stone. This notion of a substitute material is similarly seen in the adoption of Bakelite in the 1920s as a cheap and convenient imitation for such things as walnut veneer in radio sets. Although celluloid had first been produced as early as 1855, it was not until 1907 that Leo Baekeland produced phenol formaldehyde, which was suitable for the production of cheap moulded plastic imitation articles for the building trade.

Materials were frequently used by other industries long before their adoption in building construction. Aluminium, for example, was used extensively in aeronautical construction during World War II, and at the end of the war the stocks of surplus aluminium were found to be suitable as a building material, particularly for the manufacture of prefabricated houses. Similarly, neoprene was used for glazing the windscreens of vehicles for some ten years before its imaginative use by Eero Saarinen in 1953 for the first modern, gasket detailed, glass curtain wall at the General Motors Technical Centre, Detroit.

It is apparent that the inventors of these materials had no idea that the materials would be developed and used in other ways and that, given time and research, they would lead eventually, albeit via a long and complicated path, to new forms of building construction.

The second issue to consider, in the progress of new materials and techniques from inception to recognition, is the construction of a seminal building which acts as a proof of the maturity of the invention. Such buildings centre on what Machiavelli describes as 'the incredulity of mankind who do not truly believe in anything new until they have had actual experience of it'. Certain buildings have achieved this. The Benyon, Bage and Marshall Flax Spinning Mill at Ditherington, 1796–7, for example, was a landmark for cast-iron construction; the Great Stove at Chatsworth, 1836–40, for glass; the Boatstore at Sheerness, 1858–60, for functional construction; and Notre Dame, Le Raincy, 1922–3, for reinforced concrete. The actual act of construction became verification of the new material or technique. Previous buildings may have acted as test-beds for the innovation, but it was at these landmark buildings that the new material or technique was first confidently stated. These buildings appear, in retrospect, to be both an appraisal of the state of the evolutionary process and also a pointer for the future[11]. The formation of landmarks is common to most art forms. Marcell Proust provides an interesting comparison in literature.

His novel *A la Recherche du temps perdu*, which he describes as being structured like a cathedral, has become a landmark of twentieth-century literature. It manages to explore the past without reconstructing it, and also cleared the way for a new genre in literary style[12].

The tendency seems to be that landmark buildings make an impact on architectural awareness, which sets off and encourages the design and construction of a group of similar buildings. The second-generation buildings are important in the evolutionary process as they help to promote and popularize the innovatory constructional system being used.

The third issue to focus on is failure. The problem arises from the fact that, although the designers of second-generation buildings understood and copied the spirit of the innovation, they lost sight, during the design process, of the wider requirements for a successful building. Enthusiasm for the new spirit blinkered the designer so that other factors, such as the desire for comfort and the need to control condensation, were left unresolved. A clearer perspective may be gained from specific examples.

The De La Warr Pavilion at Bexhill-on-Sea (Figure 11.8) was designed in 1934 by Eric Mendelsohn and Serge Chermayeff. The building is a fine example of the Modern Movement in England following the earlier works in Germany. In spite of its importance in architectural history, the Pavilion has, since its opening, caused many problems[13]. It is apparent that some adverse criticism is due to a change in the life pattern of the users of the building, and it would be

Figure 11.8 De La Warr Pavilion, Bexhill, East Sussex, 1934; Erich Mendelsohn and Serge Chermayeff (photograph Bastiaan Valkenburg)

unfair to expect Mendelsohn and Chermayeff to have anticipated the changes in use to which the Pavilion has been subjected. Nevertheless, several other design faults have been detected. The simplified detailing of concrete, steel and glass, intended to express the Modern Movement, led to some environmental and physical defects. For example, the windows to the west staircases cause excessive solar gain, there is an unacceptable amount of wind penetration through the sundeck sliding screens, sound absorption has had to be added to the main auditorium, and the external rendering never looks tidy. The original intention was to build the Pavilion in structural concrete, but this had to be abandoned in favour of the cheaper, but less true to the Modern Movement, composite construction of a steel frame with *in-situ* concrete walling (Figure 11.9).

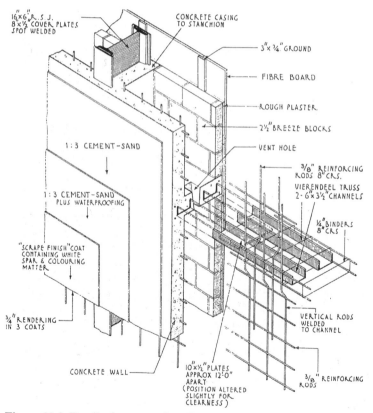

Figure 11.9 Detail of construction, De La Warr Pavilion, Bexhill, East Sussex, 1934; Erich Mendelsohn and Serge Chermayeff (reproduced from *BRE Special Report 39, Building Studies*, courtesy of the Building Research Establishment)

Another example if the Hunstanton School (Figure 11.10), built in 1949–54 by Alison and Peter Smithson. Phillip Johnson in 1954 wrote a commentary in which he referred to the design origins of the school[14]:

> For it is Mies van der Rohe who has codified the exposed steel-glass-and-brick-filled-frame grammar for us to use if we wish . . . There are additional troubles inherent in any attempt to do Mies on the cheap. One should remember the reproach often thrown at Mies: "As simple as possible, whatever the cost".

The Hunstanton School was built to meet strict cost targets and its design was energized by a desire for a fundamental expression of structure and materials (Figure 11.11). However, contemporary criticism was forthright about its construction[15]:

Figure 11.10 Hunstanton School, 1945–54; Alison and Peter Smithson (photograph Bastiaan Valkenburg)

... everywhere the exposed pipes and conduits, the black and dark brown thermoplastic floors, the unpainted, galvanized steel door frames ... the industrial, steel, light shades ... this building seems often to ignore the children for which it was built; it is hard to define if it is architecture at all.

The detailing (Figure 11.12) led to considerable problems such as condensation on the inner faces of the steel structure, excessive noise due to the absence of sound-absorbent materials, and excessive solar gain from the large areas of flat glass.

It is necessary to put the failures into perspective. Failures were sometimes followed by an emotive witch-hunt and an over-reaction. The tendency was for the whole idea to be abandoned rather than learning from an adjustment of the fault. This over-reaction helps to explain why experimental methods were often shelved and why there was often such a time lapse between invention and acceptance. it would, for example, be wrong to cast out the advantages of prefabrication in response to the various failures which led to the Ronan Point disaster of 1968, failures which have subsequently been shown to have been caused by defects in workmanship rather than in the details of construction[16]. The manufacture and use of prefabricated concrete units had evolved into a recognizable design

Figure 11.11 Corner detail, Hunstanton School, 1945–54; Alison and Peter Smithson (photograph Bastiaan Valkenburg)

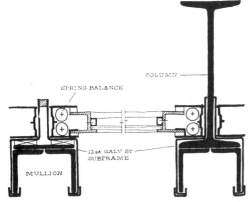

Detail shows three separate elements: 1) building frame, 2) curtain frame welded on, 3) sheet-metal window frame inserted and capped with filet.

Figure 11.12 Glazing detail, Hunstanton School, 1945–54; Alison and Peter Smithson (reproduced from *Architectural Forum*, May 1955)

language by 1968; this can be seen in the carefully detailed cladding panels of the Dining Room at St Antony's College, Oxford (Figures 11.13 and 11.14) by Howell Killick Partridge and Amis in 1966–71. Nevertheless, the effect of the Ronan Point collapse was that the use of prefabricated concrete units practically ceased, and it was not until the mid-1980s that confidence returned. This confidence was aided in 1986 by the building of Portland House, Aldermaston, Berkshire, by Richard Gilbert Scott[17]; this returned to the use of large, well-finished, prefabricated concrete units[18]. The evolutionary development of this type of construction was thus held back for over a decade.

Failure, with its costs and delays, has been part of the evolutionary process. Development has been jerky and based on empirical trial and error. The only way out of this wasteful approach is through education and research.

The evolution of research, and its present role in the design process, therefore needs to be considered. The *Strategy for Construction Research and Development* document, produced in 1985 by the Building and Civil Engineering Group of the National and Economic Development Office (NEDO), categorizes failures[19]:

Studies indicate that in building, about 50% of failure originate in the design office, about 30% on site and about 20% in materials. Clearly, the designer's role is crucial.

Are there any recurring issues within the historical surveys of this book which shed light on the reasons for such building failures?

There is, throughout the surveys, an awareness that a great deal of experimentation took place. This, however, tended to derive from vested interest in the development and promotion of a particular form of construction rather than from a collective, open-minded and objective viewpoint. The notion of an open appraisal, in the form of what we now refer to as research, was an uncommon occurrence until relatively recent times.

Andrew Saint in *Towards a Social Architecture* refers to the growth of the origins of building research[20]:

> In Britain, Edwin Sachs ought justly to be recognized as the father of the building research ideal. Betweeen 1895 and 1910, this remarkable Anglo-German architect wore himself out promoting disinterested, scientific testing of building materials. Sachs worked without government support and, as so often, only under the stress of wartime needs, and with government intervention, could further progress be made. In 1915–16, the Department of Scientific and Industrial Research came into being.

Figure 11.13 Dining Hall, St Antony's College, Oxford, 1966–71; Howell Killick Partridge and Amis (photograph Bruno de Hamel, courtesy of Howell Killick Partridge and Amis)

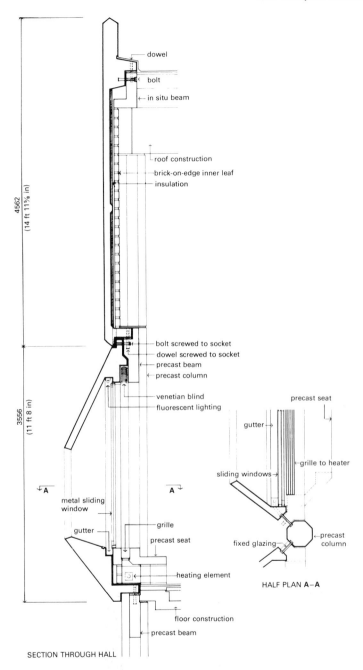

Figure 11.14 Construction detail, Dining Hall, St Antony's College, Oxford, 1966–71; Howell Killick Partridge and Amis (reproduced from *Precast Concrete Cladding*, W. R. Oram, courtesy of the British Cement Association)

This Department set up several committees to test specific building materials and systems, and the committees in turn were formed into the Building Research Station at Garston in 1924–5. The work of the Building Research Station was, however, at that time restricted to scientific analysis of materials and had little contact with architects and the design process.

The growth of modern architectural research took place during the 1930s, a century after research had become ingrained in the natural sciences and medicine, and fifty years after its adoption by the social sciences[21].The importance of architectural research as a means of anticipating and preventing failure was taken up slowly. Trevor Dannatt reflects about the time he spent in Maxwell Fry's practice during the 1930s[22]:

> A lot was built even though our building experience was limited and there was little time for reflection. We were imbued with enthusiasm, with loyalty to the practice and loyalty to the idea of architecture that Max transmitted. There was goodwill all round from clients, consultants, contractors and sub-contractors. For many years, Max declared his antipathy to professional indemnity insurance!

Many architects in the early 1930s failed to recognize that the construction industry was changing from a traditional industry, based on craft skills, to a technologically based industry. The traditional forms of construction had been based on empirical experience built up over hundreds of years; they were proven and their use required no analytical judgements. Architects in the 1930s were faced with new forms of construction and with clients who expected a higher level of comfort and control from their buildings.

Architectural research as a conscious activity began with the Tecton Group set up in 1932 by Bertold Lubetkin. This was followed by the MARS Group (Modern Architecture Research) in 1933. The first volume of *Principles of Modern Building* was published by the Building Research Station in 1938, and C. H. Waddington's influential text *The Scientific Attitude* was published in 1941. World War II encouraged some fundamental thinking. The crucial need for buildings brought with it doubts about the validity of each building being designed as a separate entity. The construction of each building as a 'prototype' was not only uneconomic but also led to frequent failures. Out of this debate came the idea of bringing together specialists from the various teams engaged on a building to set up a wide-based research unit. These became known as development groups. Andrew Saint writes[23]:

The concept of the 'developmental group' in architecture, of a small team withdrawn a little from the regular production of buildings to concentrate upon a technical task of wide application, had its origins in the pre-war and war-time enthusiasm for science, research and 'group-working' . . . it was first tried out in a backwater, the war-time offices of the London Midland and Scottish Railway . . . but Johnson-Marshall was the first to give the idea practical substance and power at the Ministry of Education's Development Group, set up in 1949.

These development groups played a vital role in the growth of system building after the war. It was from their research and through their work that many of the craft-based traditional forms of construction were replaced with new forms of industrialized construction.

Evolutionary themes

An overview of the studies demonstrates a long-term evolutionary process, from a system of heavy materials, used in load-bearing structures, to modern construction using lightweight materials assembled to exploit their tensile strength.

It is through the evolution of iron in construction that this change may be most readily perceived. A comparison between the cast iron used for early nineteenth-century mill buildings and the high tensile steels used today shows an improvement in tensile strength from $120 \, \text{N/mm}^2$ to $550 \, \text{N/mm}^2$. The visual significance of this is seen in a comparison between the span-to-depth ratios of the early iron-framed industrial mills and modern industrial buildings. A direct mathematical comparison cannot be made, owing to the change of safety factors and the introduction of elasticity into structural calculations; nevertheless, the relative structures show an evolution from a ratio of 1 to 8 at the beginning of the nineteenth century to the present figure of 1 to 18. The result is that modern structures are now far thinner and lighter. This is particularly noticeable in the work of Michael Hopkins. The lightweight and refined structural members of his Downshire Hill House at Hampstead of 1977 (Figure 11.15) would, if seen by the nineteenth-century designer, appear insubstantial and unsafe. The human requirement for a sense of containment and security is constantly being modified by the gradual change in what is visually perceived to be a safe structure.

A similar evolution is seen in the development of concrete. Here, however, the evolution was less of a straight-line pattern of growth. Over the period of a century the architectural language of reinforced concrete was established, in an evolution from the solidity of the imitation stone buildings of the 1830s to the balanced structures of Pier

Figure 11.15 Downshire Hill House, Hampstead, London, 1977; Michael Hopkins (courtesy of the Architectural Press photographic library)

Luigi Nervi in the 1930s. After World War II the use of reinforced concrete was further developed through the work of Ove Arup, who acted as engineer on several influential structures including the Brynmawr factory in Gwent, 1945–52, with the Architects Co-Partnership (Figure 11.16). The visual language of reinforced concrete was also refined by Felix Candela through such structures as the eight-petalled flower of thin paraboloids which formed the Manatiales restaurant at Xochimilco, Mexico (Figure 11.17). This he designed with the architect Joaquin Alvarez Ordoñez in 1958.

It was during this period that pre-stressed concrete began to be used. Experiments in pre-stressing had been carried out by Eugène Freyssinet in the early 1900s, followed by his patent of 1928, but it took the steel shortage after World War II to stimulate its acceptance into general practice. This had a considerable effect on the design and visual refinement of civil engineering projects. Its engineering advantages lie particularly in the design of large-span structures, and architectural potential has, to date, been largely restricted to buildings

Figure 11.16 Brynmawr Factory, Gwent, 1945–52; Architects Co-Partnership with Ove Arup (courtesy of the British Architectural Library, RIBA, London)

Figure 11.17 Mantiales Restaurant, Xochimilco, Mexico, 1958; Felix Candela with Joaquin Alvarez Ordoñez

such as bus stations and aeroplane hangars. A notable exception is the Sydney Opera House, 1957–73 (Figure 11.18) by Jørn Utzon with, again, the Ove Arup Partnership as structural engineers.

The gradual progression from heavyweight to lightweight construction is also seen in the evolution from thick load-bearing building

Figure 11.18 Sydney Opera House, 1957–73; Jørn Utzon with Ove Arup (courtesy of the British Cement Association photographic library)

Figure 11.19 Flats, 125 Park Road, Regent's Park, London, 1968; Farrell and Grimshaw (photograph James Strike)

envelopes to thinner, lightweight enclosing skins. The growth of the structural frame removed the need for heavy load-bearing masonry walls and allowed the use of lightweight cladding panels. These cladding systems developed significantly during the 1970s, and there is now a wide range of composite construction 'bolt-back' or 'clip-on' panels made from diverse materials, incorporating different types and thicknesses of insulation, and finished inside and out with an endless variation of profiles, textures, finishes and permanent colours[24].

The development of these panels began with improvements in the performance and appearance of the industrial shed. Single sheets of asbestos were replaced by double-skinned and insulated layers of aluminium. As early as 1968 Farrell and Grimshaw saw the practical advantages, and the visual potential, of using this type of construction for non-industrial buildings. In the Park Road flats (Figure 11.19) they allowed modern lightweight construction to break free from the industrial tag, and also reasserted the ideas of Jean Prouvé. New shapes and colours became available through the development of glass-reinforced plastics (GRP). An early and influential example was the headquarters building for Olivetti at Milton Keynes by Stirling and Wilford, 1969–72 (Figure 11.20). The manufacturing process and the

Figure 11.20 Headquarters building, Olivetti, Milton Keynes, 1969–72; Stirling and Wilford (reproduced from *New Architecture, Foster Rogers Stirling*, Deyan Sudjic)

strength characteristics inherent in GRP give the panels a brightly coloured smooth appearance with corrugations and two-directional curved edges: a total antithesis to the natural colour and feel of the pre-industrial earth-bound materials.

The sophistication and design vocabulary of this constructional approach is illustrated by Norman Foster's Sainsbury Centre for the Visual Arts, University of East Anglia, Norwich, 1974–7 (Figure 11.21)[25].

Figure 11.21 Sainsbury Centre for the Visual Arts, University of East Anglia, Norwich, 1974–7; Foster Associates (reproduced from *Architectural Review*, December 1978, courtesy of Foster Associates)

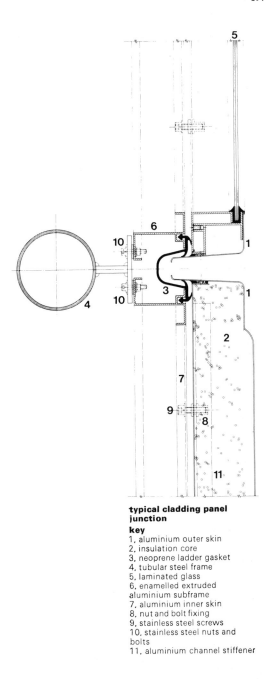

**typical cladding panel
junction**

key

1. aluminium outer skin
2. insulation core
3. neoprene ladder gasket
4. tubular steel frame
5. laminated glass
6. enamelled extruded
aluminium subframe
7. aluminium inner skin
8. nut and bolt fixing
9. stainless steel screws
10. stainless steel nuts and
bolts
11. aluminium channel stiffener

Figure 11.22 Detail of cladding, Sainsbury Centre for the Visual Arts, University of East Anglia, Norwich, 1974–7; Foster Associates (reproduced from *Architectural Review*, December 1978, courtesy of Foster Associates)

The insulated panels, faced and backed with aluminium, are bolted back to a subframe via a grid neoprene gasket (Figure 11.22). Interchangeable glazed panels can be used where necessary to promote a flexible use of the large open-plan interior (Figure 11.23). The panels form a neat and well-crafted skin over the building which speaks more of quality than of its industrial roots. The thinness of the skin is in contrast to the deep window and door reveals which gave masonry construction its visual solidity.

This sense of lightness raises another psychological problem. Is the thinness of the skin contrary to the human requirement of containment? Although the cladding to the Sainsbury Centre is equally strong and better insulated than a masonry wall, nevertheless the sense of security and protection given by the thick walls of, for example, a crofter's shelter is no longer there. The question has again to be asked: is our perception of enclosure changing as the norm of construction becomes lighter?

The issue of containment occurs also in the way that designers have made use of improved glazing systems. Improvement in the size and quality of glass, the development of hung glazing, Pilkington's Planar

Figure 11.23 Interchangeable panels, Sainsbury Centre for the Visual Arts, University of East Anglia, Norwich, 1974–7; Foster Associates (reproduced from *Architectural Review*, December 1978, courtesy of Foster Associates)

glazing and silicon-jointed glazing have all provided the designer with an extended vocabulary. This leads to areas of glazing which now have far less visually supporting substance; the appearance of openness is greater and any sense of enclosure minimal. The apparently unsupported and unframed glass envelope of, for example, the Willis Faber Dumas Headquarters in Ipswich by Foster Associates (Figure 11.24) created enthusiastic wonder in 1975. The glazing at Ipswich was designed by Martin Francis, who further pursued the potential of minimalist glazing for the vast glazed boxes at the City of Science and Industry, La Villette, Paris, 1986 (Figures 11.25 and 11.26). The glazing at La Villette also demonstrates the influence which the high-tensile constructional detailing of, for example, modern racing yachts has had on the art of glazing. This influence has been aided by the work of Richard Horden through his exploratory detailing for the New Forest House of 1982 (Figure 11.27).

Another long-term evolutionary theme in construction which has influenced design has been the development of prefabrication. The gradual increase in the size of units which could be manoeuvred economically has led to a change of visual grain in the design of buildings. A look at the extremes of the spectrum helps to reveal the degree of change. Prior to the Industrial Revolution the normal unit of preformed building material was the length of timber, the cut stone or the moulded brick. The assembly of these gave, through the lines of their joints, a close-grained appearance. In the case of brickwork, the joints are so close and regular that they form a texture. Today, the unit of pre-formed building material is larger and the visual grain wider, as can be seen, for example, in the distinct joint marks in the elevation of the Universal Oil Products Fragrances Factory, 1973, by Renzo Piano and Richard Rogers (Figure 11.28). The potential was further realized by the large preformed stainless steel[26] service units stacked in the external towers of the Lloyd's Building, 1978–86, by Richard Rogers and Partners (Figure 11.29). The effect is a change from the monolithic appearance and close-grained texture of brickwork or stone to the digital and additive appearance of large preformed building units.

The question now being asked is: how does the move from heavy monolithic construction to lightweight construction affect what Colin Rowe refers to as 'Phenomena Transparency'[27], the idea that the outward appearance of a building portrays a mental vision of its internal architecture? Does the change from a thick and solid to a thin and lightweight facade alter the way the interior is perceived?

Figure 11.24 Willis Faber Dumas Headquarters Building, Ipswich, Suffolk, 1975; Foster Associates (photograph Bastiaan Valkenburg)

Figure 11.25 Glazing, City of Science and Industry, La Villette, Paris, 1986; Martin Francis (reproduced from *Building Design*, Window and Glazing Supplement 1986)

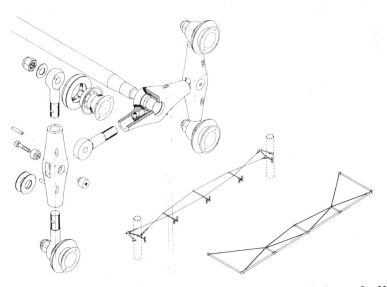

Figure 11.26 Construction of glazing, City of Science and Industry, La Villette, Paris, 1986; Martin Francis (reproduced from *Building Design*, Window and Glazing Supplement 1986)

Figure 11.27 New Forest House, 1982; Richard Horden (reproduced from *Building Design*, 15 March 1985)

Figure 11.28 Universal Oil Products Fragrances Factory, Tadworth, Surrey, 1973; Renzo Piano and Richard Rogers (photograph Richard Einzig, courtesy of ARCAID)

Figure 11.29 Lloyd's Building, Leadenhall, City of London, 1986–7; Richard Rogers Partnership (photograph James Strike)

Conclusion

There arises from this appraisal the notion that construction can be used as a medium for architectural criticism. Recurring through the study has been the perception that the architectural quality of a building is related to the way in which it is put together; the idea that the architectural quality of a building may be judged through the characteristics of its construction. This goes beyond an assessment of the quality of craftsmanship, as it includes judgements on the suitability of materials, the suitability of structure [28], the representational qualities of the materials and construction, the coherence of detailing, and a general awareness of the morphology of the building.

This approach is seen in Gustave Flaubert's passion for the aesthetic power of words. He would spend days on a single page of manuscript and he declared that '. . . when I displace a word I sometimes have to change several pages'. There was a perpetual struggle for the appropriate word [29]. Similarities can also be seen in the role which metre plays in Shakespeare, the descriptive grain of Dickens or the structure of a plot by John le Carré.

An understanding of the position of a building in history, and of the roots of its materials and construction, helps in this assessment of the qualities of the building as a piece of architecture. The Crystal Palace can thus be seen as a synthesis of the cast-iron skeleton frames of the early mill buildings and the glazing techniques of the early conservatory hothouses. Similarly, the Eames House may be perceived within the perspective of the Functional Tradition, the constructional experiments of the Bauhaus and early types of system construction. The idea emerges that 'chains of influences' exist through history, which, when seen in retrospect, help to identify the origins of a type of construction. It is this understanding which assists in our criticism of modern architecture.

Looking at an example, Nicholas Grimshaw's houses on the Grand Union Canal, 1989 (Figure 11.30) can thus be seen as a natural continuation of the chain: the iron facades of James Bogardus of the late 1840s, the early iron-clad naval craft of the 1860s, the metal facades of Paris at the turn of the century, the development of metal-faced prefabricated panels by the Bauhaus team in the early 1930s, the lightweight metal structures of Jean Prouvé in the late

Figure 11.30 Houses on the Grand Canal, Camden, London, 1989; Nicholas Grimshaw (photograph James Strike)

Figure 11.31 Terminal Building, Stansted Airport, 1988–90; Foster Associates

1930s, the introduction of gasket jointing in the 1950s, and the development of lightweight cladding system in the 1970s.

Similarly, the Terminal Building at Stansted Airport, 1988–90, by Norman Foster (Figure 11.31) can be seen to have its pedigree in the rational construction of the early industrial mills, particularly in the work of Alexander and Rennie at Tobacco Dock, Wapping (Figure 1.15).

Seeing modern buildings in terms of their ancestral trees is a useful form of architectural criticism.

Finally, it has to be noted that several issues arise which, although important in their own right, do not fall within the scope of this book. Particularly important this need to regenerate and coordinate the funding and application of research, and the need to reappraise the teaching of building construction within the schools. It is necessary to reduce the number of failures in the building industry and also to improve the quality of built architecture through a clearer understanding of the significance of the historical evolution of construction.

APPENDIX CHRONOLOGICAL LISTING

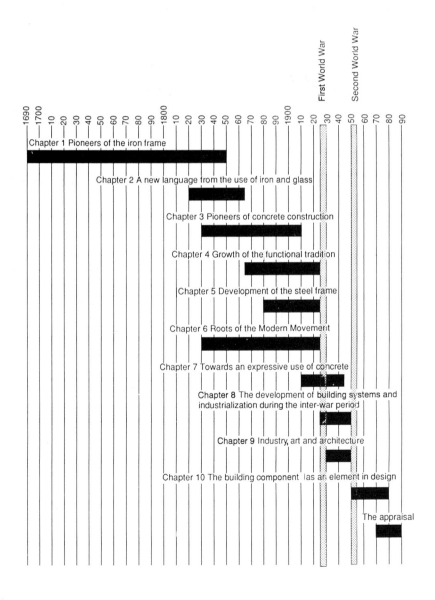

First World War

Second World War

1690 1700 10 20 30 40 50 60 70 80 90 1800 10 20 30 40 50 60 70 80 90 1900 10 20 30 40 50 60 70 80 90

Chapter 1 Pioneers of the iron frame

Chapter 2 A new language from the use of iron and glass

Chapter 3 Pioneers of concrete construction

Chapter 4 Growth of the functional tradition

Chapter 5 Development of the steel frame

Chapter 6 Roots of the Modern Movement

Chapter 7 Towards an expressive use of concrete

Chapter 8 The development of building systems and industrialization during the inter-war period

Chapter 9 Industry, art and architecture

Chapter 10 The building component as an element in design

The appraisal

BIBLIOGRAPHY

Academy Editions, 1982, *K. F. Schinkel, Collected Architectural Editions*.

Act of Parliament, 1944, *Housing (Temporary Accommodation) Act*, HMSO.

Aldridge, H. J., 1923, *The National Housing Manual*, National Housing and Town Planning Council, HMSO.

Allan, John, February 1988, 'The Penguin Pool, London Zoo', *RIBA Journal*.

Allen, A. H., 1978, *Prestressed Concrete*, Cement and Concrete Association.

Aluminium Development Association, 1948, *The First Factory-Made Aluminium Bungalow*, The Aluminium Federation.

Architect and Building News, February 15 1935, 'Factory-made architecture. Flats at Drancy, near Paris. Architects: Eugène Beaudoin and Marcel Lods'.

Architectural Forum, November 1954, 'General Motors Technical Centre'.

Architectural Forum, May 1955, 'Secondary School, Hunstanton'.

Architectural Journal, 29 October 1986, 'Objectors plead for Brynmawr Factory'.

Architectural Record, February 1939, 'New structural system reduces site fabrication to a minimum. Eugène Mopin, Engineer'.

Arup Partnership, 1982, *Appraisal of Existing Ferrous Metal Structures*.

Baddensieg, Tilmann, translated by White, *Industriekultur, Peter Behrens and the AEG*, MIT Press.

Banham, Reyner, 1969, *The Architecture of the Well-Tempered Environment*, Architectural Press.

Banham, Reyner, 1960, *Theory and Design in the First Machine Age*, Architectural Press.

Bannister, Turpin, April 1960, 'The first iron-framed buildings', *Architectural Review*.

Beckford, William, 1835, *Recollections of an Excursion to the Monasteries of Alcobaça and Batalha*, R. Bently, London.

Behrens, Peter, 12 February 1910, 'The Turbine Hall of the AEG building at Berlin', *Deutsche Techniker-Zeitung 27*, No.6.

Benson, A. C., Jones, F. M. and Vaughan, J. E., June 1963, 'Early example of prefabrication', *RIBA Journal*.

Benton, Tim, *Peter Behrens and the AEG Company*, Video, Open University Course, History of Architecture and Design 1890–1939, Course Index A305.

Berlage, H. P., 1908, *Grundlagen und Entwicklung der Architektur*.

Berliner Tegeblatt, 29 August 1907 (evening edition), Interview with Peter Behrens on his appointment as artistic adviser to the AEG company.

Bird, Anthony, 1976, *Paxton's Palace*, Cassell.

Boesiger, W., 1960, *Le Corbusier 1910–60*, Alec Tiranti.

Bossom, Alfred, 1934, *Building to the Skies*, The Studio Press.

Boudon, Philippe, 1969, *Lived-in Architecture: Le Corbusier's Pessac Revisited*, Lund Humphries.

Boyne, Colin, September 1954, 'Hunstanton School', *Architects Journal*.

Bucknell, L. H., 1935, *Industrial Architecture*, Whitefriars Press.

Building Design, 20 November 1981, 'The Pavilion A1, Brno, Czechoslovakia'.

Building Research Station, 1938, *Principles of Modern Building*, Vol.1, HMSO.

Cantacuzino, Sherban, 1981, *Howell Killick Partridge and Amis: architecture*, Lund Humphries.

Carlyle, Thomas, 1829 'Signs of the times', in Alisdair Clayre (ed.), 1977, *Nature and Industrialization*, Oxford University Press.

Chadwick, George F., 1961, *The Works of Sir Joseph Paxton 1803–65*, Architectural Press.

Choisy, Auguste, 1899, *Histoire de l'Architecture*, Paris.

Civil Engineer and Architects Journal, 1850, 'Details of Paxton's Roofing'.

CLASP, 1961, *The Story of CLASP*, Building Bulletin 19, Ministry of Education, HMSO.

CLASP, 1965, *Annual Report: Report of Eight Years Work*, HMSO.

Clayre, Alisdair (ed.), 1977, *Nature and Industrialization*, Oxford University Press.

Clifton-Taylor, Alec, 1962, *The Pattern of English Building*, Faber and Faber.

Coad, Jonathan, 1983, *The Historic Architecture of the Royal Navy*, Victor Gollanz.

Cole, Henry (ed.), 1849, *Journal of Design*. Special Book Collection, V and A Museum.

Collins, Peter, 1959, *Concrete, a Vision of a New Architecture*, Faber and Faber.

Colquhoun, Alan, November 1962, 'Symbolic and literal aspects of technology', *Architectural Design*.

Corbusier, Le, 1923, *Vers une Architecture*, Vincent, Paris. Translated by Frederick Etchells.

Cottam, David, 1986, *Owen Williams 1890–1969*, Architectural Association.

Dannatt, Trevor, October 1987, 'Edwin Maxwell Fry 1899–1987', *The Architect*.

Dean, David, 1983, *The Thirties: Recalling the English Architectural Scene*, Trefoil Books.

Dickinson, H. W., 1954, *Water Supply of Greater London*, Newcomen Society.

Diestelkamp, E. J., July–September 1982, Design and building of the Palm House, Kew, *Journal of Gardening History*.

Dinardo, C., 17 May 1988, The Uniroyal Factory, Dumfries, *The Structural Engineer*.

Dixon, Roger and Muthesius, Stefan, 1978, *Victorian Architecture*, Thames and Hudson.

Downes, Charles, 1852, *The Building Erected in Hyde Park for the Great Exhibition*.

Enticknapp, Judy, 1983, *Nineteenth Century Conservatories*, Dissertation for MA in Conservation Studies, Institute of Advanced Architectural Studies, York University.

Fitzgerald, R., 1977, 'Save British Heritage', in *Satanic Mills*.

Forty, Adrian, 1986, *Objects of Desire: Design and Society 1750–1980*. Thames and Hudson.

Foster, Michael, 1983, *The Principles of Architecture, Style, Structure and Design*, Phaidon.

Frampton, Kenneth, 1980, *Modern Architecture, A Critical History*, Thames and Hudson.

Garnier, Tony, 1917, *Une Cité Industrielle*. Translated by Dora Wiebenson, 1969, Studio Vista.

Ginzburg, Moisei, *Stil'i Epokha*, 1924. Translated by Anatole Senkevitch, 1982, *Style and Epoch*, MIT Press.

Gloag, John and Bridgwater, Derek, 1948, *A History of Cast Iron in Architecture*, George Allen and Unwin.

Gloag, John, 1970, *Mr Loudon's London*, Oriel Press.

Goldburger, Paul, 1981, *The Skyscraper*, Knopf, New York.

Gomme, Andor and Walker, David, 1968, *Architecture of Glasgow*, Lund Humphries

Goodhart-Rendel, H. S., 1924, *Nicholas Hawksmoor*, Ernest Benn.

Government Command Paper, 1918, *Building Byelaws, Report of the Local Government Board Committee, Cd. 9213*. HMSO.

Government Command Paper, 1945, *Housing, Cd. 6609*, HMSO.

Granville, A. B., 1841, *The Spas of England and the Principal Sea-Bathing Places*.

Gropius, Walter, 1935, *The New Architecture of the Bauhaus*, Faber.

Grunfeld, Frederick, 1977, *Berlin*, Time Life.

Guadet, Julien, *Eléments et Théories de l'Architecture, Libraire de la Construction Moderne*, Paris.

Handlin, David P., 1985, *American Architecture*, Thames and Hudson.

Heath, G. D., 1979, *The Chapel Royal at Hampton Court*, Twickenham Local History Society, Paper No 2.

Herbert, Gilbert, 1978, *Pioneers of Prefabrication, The British Contribution in the Nineteenth Century*, Johns Hopkins University Press.

Hix, John, 1974, *The Glass House*, Phaidon Press.

HMSO, Post-war Building Studies No.1, *House Construction*.

Hodgkinson, 1830, *Theoretical and Experimental Research to Ascertain the Strength and Best Form of Cast Iron Beams*, paper presented to the Manchester Literary and Philosophical Society.

Housing, 16 August 1920, *A Report on the Waller System*, HMSO.

Huber, B. and Steinegger, J. C., (eds), 1971, *Jean Prouvé, Prefabrication, Structures and Elements*, Pall Mall Press.

Hudnut, Joseph, May 1945, 'The Post Modern House', *Architectural Record*.

Hughes, Quentin J., 1969, *Liverpool*, City Building Series, Studio Vista.

Huxtable, Ada Louise, 1982, *The Tall Building Artistically Reconsidered*, Pantheon Books.

Illustrated London News, March 1856, 'The Gardner's Store, Glasgow'.

Jackson, Anthony, 1970, *The Politics of Architecture*, Architectural Press.

James, M. A. I., *The Weaver's Mill, Swansea*, Thesis, Open University, Ref DO.111526.

Jandl, H. Ward (ed.), 1983, *The Technology of Historic American Buildings: Studies of the Materials, Craft Processes, and the Mechanization of Building Conservation*, The Association for Preservation Technology, Washington, DC.

Johnson, Phillip,, September 1954, 'Commentary on the Hunstanton School', *Architectural Review*.

Jones, Edgar, 1985, *Industrial Architecture in Britain 1750–1939*, Batsford.

Khan-Mahomedor, S. O., February 1970, 'Building in the USSR 1917–1932', *Architectural Design*.

Knevitt, Charles, 5 September 1986, 'Ronan Point, bad workmanship found', in *The Times*.

Lethaby, William, 1922, *Form in Civilization*, Oxford University Press.

Lissitzky, El, 1920, *Proun, Not World Vision, But World Reality*, in Sophie Lissitzky-Kuppers, 1968, *El Lissitzky, Life, Letters and Texts*, Thames and Hudson.

Lloyd, David W., 1974, *Buildings of Portsmouth and its Environments*, City of Portsmouth Publications.

Loudon, J. S., 1822, *An Encyclopaedia of Gardening*, London.

Loudon, J. S., 1833, *An Encyclopaedia of Cottage Farm and Villa Architecture*, London.

Lyall, Sutherland, 1980, *The State of British Architecture*, Architectural Press.

Machiavelli, N., *The Prince*. Translated by Marriott, 1914, J. M. Dent.

Mallinson, L. G., 1986, *An Historical Examination of Concrete*, D.O.E. Report DOE/RW/86/097.

March, Lionel and Steadman, Philip, 1974, *The Geometry of the Environment*, Methuen.

Maré, Eric de, 1973, *The Nautical Style*, Architectural Press.

Mead, Martin, July 1988, 'Iron in the soul', *Architectural Review*.

Miller, Philip, 1988, *Decimus Burton 1800–1881*, The Building Centre Trust.

Ministry of Reconstruction, 1919, *Housing in England and Wales*, Pamphlet No 7, Pamphlets on Reconstruction Problems, HMSO.

Moholy-Nagy, L., *From Materials to Architecture*, in Krisztina Passuth, *Moholy-Nagy*, Thames and Hudson.

Moszynska, Anna, 1990, *Abstract Art*, Thames and Hudson.

Mouchel, L. G., 1921, *Hennebique Ferro-Concrete, Theory and Practice*, L. G. Mouchel and Partners.

Muche, George, 1926, 'Fine Art and Industrial Form', *The Bauhaus Journal*.

Mujica, Francisco, 1929, *History of the Skyscraper*, Archaeology and Architectural Press, Paris, at the RIBA special collection.

Mumford, Lewis, *The Brown Decades, A Study of the Arts in America 1865–1895*.

Muthesius, Hermann, 3 July 1914, *The Task of the Werkbund in the Future*, Open University; A305D.

Muthesius, Hermann, 1904–5, *Das Englishe Haus*. Translated by Janet Seligman, 1979, Crosby Lockwood Staples.

National Building Studies, 1966, *Special Report 39, Qualitative Studies of Buildings*, HMSO.

National Economic Development Office, 1985, *Strategy for Construction, Research and Development*, Building and Civil Engineering EDC.

Naylor, Gillian, 1985, *The Bauhaus Reassessed*, Herbert Press.

Nervi, Pier Luigi, 1956 (translated by Giuseppina and Mario Salvadori), *Structures*, F. W. Dodge.

Nervi, Pier Luigi and Rogers, Ernesto, 1957, *The Works of Pier Luigi Nervi*, Architectural Press.

Nissen, Henrik, 1972, *Industrialized Building and the Modular Design*, Cement and Concrete Association.

O'Gorman, James F., February 1970, 'A Bogardus Original', *Architectural Review*.

Oram, W. R., 1978, *Precast Concrete Cladding*, Cement and Concrete Association.

Ostler, Tim, 1986, *Art of Glass*, in Building Design Supplement: Doors, Windows and Glazing.

Pacey, A. J., February 1969, 'Earliest cast iron beams', *Architectural Review*.

Palladio, Andrea, 1570, *Four Books of Architecture* (Isaac Ware Edition, 1738, Dover Publications)

Passuth, Krisztina, 1985, *Maholy-Nagy*, Thames and Hudson.

Pehnt, Wolfgang, 1973, *Expressionist Architecture*, Thames and Hudson.

Penoyre, John and Jane, 1978, *Houses in the Landscape*, Faber and Faber.

Perkin, George, April 1986, 'Lakeside Headquarters', *Concrete Quarterly*.

Pevsner, Nikolaus, 1936, *Pioneers of Modern Design from William Morris to Walter Gropius*, Pelican.

Pevsner, Nikolaus, 1956, *The Englishness of English Art*, Penguin.

Pevsner, Nikolaus, 1969, *South Lancashire, Buildings of England*, Penguin.

Physick, John, 1982, *The Victoria and Albert Museum. The History of its Building*, V and A publication.

Posener, Julius, 1972, *From Schinkel to the Bauhaus*, Architectural Association Paper 5, Lund Humphries.

Posener, Julius, 1979, *Hermann Muthesius 1861–1927*, Architectural Association.

Powell, C. G., 1980, *An Economic History of the British Building Industry 1815–1979*, Methuen.

Pritchard, Jack, January 1969, 'Gropius, the Bauhaus and the future', *Journal of the Royal Society of Arts*.

Pugin and Rowlandson, 1904, *The Microcosm of London*, Founded on the Original Edition by Rudolph Ackermann, Methuen.

Relph-Knight, Lynda, 27 January 1984, 'Flexible futures', *Building Design*.

Relph-Knight, Lynda, 15 March 1985, 'Nautical lines', *Building Design*.

RIBA Journal, October 1974, 'Park Road Flats by Farrell and Grimshaw'.

Richards, J. M., 1968, *The Functional Tradition*, Architectural Press.

Robson, Robert (ed.), *c*.1860, *The Mason's, Bricklayer's, Plasterer's and Decorator's Practical Guide*, London

Rowe, Colin, 1976, 'Literal and phenomena transparency', in *The Mathematics of the Ideal Villa and other Essays*, Cambridge, Mass.

Ruskin, John, 1853, *The Stones of Venice*, London.

Ruskin, John, 1853, *The Seven Lamps of Architecture*, London.

Russell, Barry, 1981, *Building Systems, Industrialization and Architecture*, John Wiley and Sons.

Saint, Andrew, 1983, *The Image of The Architect*, Yale University Press.

Saint, Andrew, 1987, *Towards a Social Architecture, The Role of Post-War School Building in England*, Yale University Press.

Schomaekers, G., 1976, *The American Civil War*, Blandford Press.

Schubert, H. R., 1957, *History of the British Iron and Steel Industry from 450 BC to 1775 AD*, Routledge and Kegan Paul.

Schulze, Franz, 1985, *Mies van der Rohe, A Critical Biography*, University of Chicago Press.

Scott, Geoff, 1976, *Building Disasters*, The Construction Press.

Semper, Gottfried, 1852, *Wissenschaft, Industrie und Kunst.*

Senkevitch, Anatole, 1974, *Soviet Architecture 1917–1962. A Bibliographical Guide to Source Material*, University Press of Virginia, USA.

Service, Alistair, 1977, *Edwardian Architecture*, Thames and Hudson.

Sharp, Dennis, *Mendelsohn and the Einstein Tower*, Video, Open University Course, History of Architecture and Design 1890–1939, Course Index A305.

Sharp, Dennis, 1966, *Modern Architecture and Expressionism*, Longman.

Sharp, Dennis, 1972, *A Visual History of Twentieth Century Architecture*, Heinemann/Socker and Warburg.

Smithson, Alison and Peter, 1981, *The Heroic Period of Modern Architecture*, Thames and Hudson.

Smithson, Alison and Peter, 1982, *Alison and Peter Smithson, The Shift*, Architectural Monograph 7, Academy Editions.

Stanley, Christopher, 1979, *Highlights in the History of Concrete*, Cement and Concrete Association.

Steele, H and Yerbury, F. R., 1930, *The Old Bank of England*, Ernest Benn.

Stroud, Dorothy, 1984, *Sir John Soane, Architect*, Faber and Faber.

Sudjic, Deyan, 1986, *New Architecture: Foster Rogers Stirling*, Royal Academy of Arts.

Sullivan, Louis, *The Tall Office Building Artistically Considered.*

Sunley, John and Beddington, Barbara (eds), 1985, *Timber in Construction*, Batsford and TRADA.

The Times, 27 June 1850, article on the Crystal Palace.

Thorne, Robert (ed.), 1990, *The Iron Revolution*, RIBA.

Tilson, Barbara, 4 December 1987, 'Form and function', *Building Design.*

de Tocqueville, Alexis, 1835, *Joruneys to England and Ireland*, in Alisdair Clayre (ed.), 1977, *Nature and Industrialization*, Oxford University Press in association with Open University Press.

Torroja, Eduardo, 1958, *The Structures of Eduardo Torroja*, F. W. Dodge.

Tregold, Thomas, 1820, *Elementary Principles of Carpentry.*

Trinder, Barrie, 1979, *The Iron Bridge*, Iron Bridge Museum Trust, Museum Guide 3.01.

Tudor, G. D. C., March 31 1988, 'Brunel's Private Kingdom', *Country Life.*

Venturi, Robert, 1966, *Complexity and Contradiction in Architecture*, New York.

Waddington, C. H., 1941, *The Scientific Attitude*, Penguin.

Ware, Isaac, 1768, *A Complete Body of Architecture*, Gregg International.

Wayss, G. A., 1887, *Monierbau*.

Walker, Derek, 1987, *Great Engineers*, Academic Editions and Royal College of Art.

Wells, John, 1987, *The Immortal Warrior, Britain's First and Last Battleship*, Kenneth Mason.

White, R. B., 1965, *Prefabrication. A History of Its Development in Great Britain*, Ministry of Technology, National Building Studies, Special Report 36, Building Research Station, HMSO.

Whyte, Ian Boyd, 1985, *Otto Wagner*, Museum of Modern Art, Oxford.

Windsor, Alan, 1981, *Peter Behrens, Architect and Designer 1868–1940*, Architectural Press.

Winter, John, 1970, *Industrial Architecture, A Survey of Factory Buildings*, Studio Vista.

Wyatt, Matthew Digby, 1851, 'The Crystal Palace', *Journal of Design*, Special Book Collection, V and A Museum.

NOTES AND REFERENCES

Introduction
1. Ruskin, 1853, *The Stones of Venice*, Chapter 2, The Virtues of Architecture, p.1.
2. Nervi, 1956, *Structures*, p.1.
3. Palladio, 1570, *Quattro Libri dell'Architettura*, first English translation by Isaac Ware, 1738.
4. Ibid., preface, p.2.
5. Ibid, preface, p.2.
6. Choisy, 1899, *Histoire de l'Architecture*.
7. Banham, 1960, *Theory and Design in the First Machine Age*, Chapter 2, Choisy, Rationalism and Technique.
8. Pevsner, 1936, *Pioneers of Modern Design*.
9. Venturi, 1966, *Complexity and Contradiction in Architecture*.

Chapter 1
1. Schubert, 1975, *History of the British Iron and Steel Industry from 450 BC to 1775 AD*.
2. Ware, 1768, *A Complete Body of Architecture*, p.89.
3. Clifton-Taylor, 1962, *The Pattern of English Building*, p.387.
4. Schubert, 1975, *History of the British Iron and Steel Industry from 450 BC to 1775 AD*.
5. Gloag and Bridgwater, 1948, *A History of Cast Iron in Architecture*, p.115.
6. Sunley and Bedding (eds), 1985, *Timber in Construction*, Chapter 5.
7. This became known as 'Tredgold's Tables' and was in use up to the 1940s.
8. Meade, 1988, *Iron in the Soul*.
9. For example, restoration of the Customs House, Dublin (James Gandon, 1791), revealed bands of 50-mm square section iron

reinforcement through the masonry above each row of windows and through the entablature. The building was gutted by fire in 1922, causing the iron bars to expand and damage the stonework. Structural analysis has shown that these iron bands do not contribute to the stability of the building and they have now been removed.

10. Dickinson, 1954, *The Water Supply of London*.
11. Pugin and Rowlandson, 1904, *The Microcosm of London*.
12. Beckford, *Recollections of an Excursion to the Monasteries of Alcobaça and Batalha*.
13. In *The First Iron-Framed Buildings*, Turpin Banister.
14. Stroud, 1984, *Sir John Soane Architect*, p.153.
15. Research by Dr Ivan Hall (English Heritage) shows that there was an earlier iron bridge built by Maurice Tobin in 1769 at Kirklees Pass, Huddersfield. This was demolished later in the eighteenth century. It is not known whether this was constructed in wrought or cast iron. It was a bowstring pattern with timber decking spanning 21 metres.
16. Coad, 1983, *Historic Architecture of the Royal Navy*, p.39.
17. Fitzgerald, 1977, *Save British Heritage*.
18. Pacey, 1969, *Earliest Cast Iron Beams*.
19. As (8).
20. The French physicist, Charles Coulomb, established in 1773 the correct relationship between the bending moment and the moment of resistance in beams: the Swiss scientist, Bernoulli, in 1694 applied Mariotte's law to determine deflection; the French physicist, Edme Mariotte, in 1680 demonstrated that compression took place at the top of the beam and compression at the bottom; and Robert Hooke established the elasticity of solids in 1678.
21. Thome (ed.) *The Iron Revolution*, p.26.
22. Particularly the Reverend Edmund Cartwright's power loom patented in 1785, 6 and 7.
23. Clayre (ed.), 1977, *Nature and Industrialization*, p.229.
24. Ibid., p.117.
25. Penoyre and Penoyre, 1978, *Houses in the Landscape*.
26. Pevsner, 1936, *Pioneers of Modern Design*, p.121.
27. Posener, 1972, *From Schinkel to the Bauhaus*.
28. Blake, 1804, *Milton*, preface.

Chapter 2
1. The tie-rods at the head of the columns were added later.
2. Hughes, 1969, Liverpool, p.24.

3. Lloyd, 1974, *Buildings of Portsmouth*, p.122.
4. Gloag, 1970, *Mr Loudon's London*, Chapter 4.
5. Hix, 1974, *The Glass House*, p.22.
6. Loudon, 1833, *An Encyclopaedia of Cottage, Farm and Villa Architecture*.
7. Mead, 1988, *Iron in the Soul*, p.7.
8. Granville, 1841, *The Spas of England and the Principal Sea-bathing Places*.
9. Peterson, 1987, *Inventing the I-beam*, in Jandl H. Ward (ed.), 1987, *Technology of Historic American Buildings*, p.66.
10. Diestelkamp, 1982, *Design and Building of the Palm House, Kew*.
11. Dixon and Muthesius, 1978, *Victorian Architecture*, p.98.
12. This replaced an earlier shed of 1836, and was replaced in 1867 by the third shed.
13. O'Gorman, 1970, *A Bogardus Original*.
14. Bird, 1976, *Paxton's Palace*, p.22.
15. Dixon and Muthesius, 1978, *Victorian Architecture*, p.102.
16. Miller, 1981, *Decimus Burton*, p.43.
17. Tudor, 1988, *Brunel's Private Kingdom*.
18. Pevsner, 1936, *Pioneers of Modern Design*, p.133.
19. Ruskin, 1853, *The Seven Lamps of Architecture*, Chapter 2.

Chapter 3
1. Mallinson, 1986, *An Historical Examination of Concrete*, p.37.
2. The use of stucco work to replicate stone became comon practice in Italy during the sixteenth century. A notable example was the work of Giulio Romano in Mantua (see Palazzo del Te, *c*.1533, and Cortile della Cavallerizza, 1538–39). In Britain examples do exist earlier than the 1770s, one of the earliest being Lunday House, a red brick house built in the 1640s with windows and doors trimmed with stucco false ashlar.
3. An early use was at Kenwood House, Hampstead, London, 1778.
4. Manufactured by J. B. White and Sons at Swanscombe, Kent. Parker's patent was bought out by James Wyatt in 1810.
5. An early use was for Regent's Park Terrace, London.
6. Mallinson, 1986, *An Historical Examination of Concrete*, p.25, refers to Joseph Aspdin, a young bricklayer in Leeds, purchasing a copy of *A Narrative of the Eddystone Lighthouse*. This contained an account of John Smeaton's experiments with cements which led him to retain the use of pozzolana. This started Aspdin in his search for an improved hydraulic cement.

7. Stanley, 1979, *Highlights in the History of Concrete*, p.11.
8. Ibid., p.23.
9. Ibid., p.18.
10. Concrete workers from France were used on site.
11. James, *The Weaver and Company Provender Mill, Swansea*.
12. The building was altered in 1939, the window heights were reduced and a modern type of industrial window installed.

Chapter 4
1. Pevsner, 1956, *The Englishness of English Art*, Chapter 3.
2. Collins, 1959, *Concrete, a Vision of a New Architecture*.
3. Physick, 1982, *The Victoria and Albert Museum, The History of its Building*, p.22.
4. Ibid., p.23.
5. Ibid., pp.24 and 25.
6. Ibid., p.24.
7. Arup Partnership, 1982, *Appraisal of Existing Ferrous Metal Structures*, p.5.
8. Winter, 1970, *Industrial Architecture, A Survey of Factory Buildings*, p.69.
9. Richards, 1968, *The Functional Tradition*, p.59.
10. This was preceded by the French ironclad *La Gloire* of 1858.
11. Wells, 1987, *The Immortal Warrior, Britain's First and Last Battleship*, p.42.
12. Gomme and Walker, 1968, *Architecture of Glasgow*.
13. Lion Chambers was built using a Mouchel-Hennebique ferro-concrete structure.
14. The factory is currently being renovated by Dinardo and Partners, Dinardo, 1988, *The Uniroyal Factory*, Dumfries.

Chapter 5
1. Arup Partnership, 1982, *Appraisal of Existing Ferrous Metal Structures*, p.13.
2. Foster (ed.), 1983, *The Principles of Architecture, Style, Structure and Design*, p.116.
3. Ibid., p.117.
4. Goldburger, 1981, *The Skyscraper*.
5. Mumford, 1931, *The Brown Decades, A Study of the Arts in America 1865–1895*.
6. Bossom, 1934, *Building to the Skies*, p.121.
7. Ibid., Chapter 6.
8. Forty, 1986, *Objects of Desire: Design and Society 1750–1980*.

Chapter 6
1. Smithson and Smithson, 1981, *The Heroic Period of Modern Architecture*, p.9.
2. Sharp, 1972, *A Visual History of Twentieth Century Architecture*.
3. Quoted from Posener, 1972, *From Schinkel to the Bauhaus*, p.11.
4. Ibid., p.12.
5. Schulze, 1985, *Mies van der Rohe, A Critical Biography*.
6. Frampton, 1980, *Modern Architecture, A Critical History*, p.109.
7. Posener, 1972, *From Schinkel to the Bauhaus*, p.18.
8. Muthesius, 1904–5, *Das Englische Haus*.
9. Notably the Glasgow Herald building, 1893; the Glasgow School of Art, east wing, 1897–9; the Daily Record Office, 1901.
10. Windsor, 1981, *Peter Behrens, Architect and Designer 1868–1940*, p.54.
11. Written in 1958.
12. Posener, 1972, *From Schinkel to the Bauhaus*, p.23.
13. Lethaby, 1922, *Form in Civilization*.
14. Windsor, 1981, *Peter Behrens, Architect and Designer 1868–1940*, p.53.
15. Translation from Buddensieg, *Industriekultur*.
16. *Deutsch Techniker-Zeitung* 27, No.6, 12 February 1910.
17. Benton, *Peter Behrens and the AEG Company*.
18. Gropius, 1935, *The New Architecture of the Bauhaus*, p.47.
19. Gropius, 1935, *The New Architecture of the Bauhaus*, p.19.
20. Schulz, 1985, *Mies van der Rohe, A Critical Biography*, also comments that only Adolf Loos had previously achieved this with the solid cube of the Steinerk House in Vienna, 1910.
21. Muthesius, 1914, *The Task of the Werkbund in the Future*.

Chapter 7
1. Built to commemorate the rising against Napoleon in 1813.
2. Unsurpassed, even by the ingenuity of Brunelleschi's dome for Florence Cathedral and Michelangelo's dome for St Peter's, Rome.
3. Pehnt, 1973, *Expressionist Architecture*.
4. Sharp, *Mendelsohn and the Einstein Tower*.
5. Translation by Wiebenson.
6. Owen Williams was chief designer for the Trussed Concrete Steel Company between 1912 and 1916. The company was later named Truscon. See Cottam 1986, *Owen Williams*, p.80.
7. One of the first uses in Britain.

8. Mario Salvadori, in Nervi, 1956, *Structures*.
9. Nervi, 1956, *Structures*.
10. Ibid.
11. Torroja, 1958, *The Structures of Eduardo Torroja*.

Chapter 8

1. Followed in 1600 BC by the movement of the great Sarsen stones, each weighing about 50 tonnes, from the Marlborough Downs, some 32 km north of Stonehenge.
2. Heath, 1979, *The Chapel Royal at Hampton Court*, p.6.
3. John Alexander Brodie was an early partner in the firm of consulting engineers now known as Parkman. He left the firm in 1898 to become City Engineer of Liverpool, a post he held until 1926.
4. Benson, Jones and Vaughan, 1963, *Early Examples of Prefabrication*.
5. White, 1965, *Ministry of Technology: National Building Studies: Special Report 36*, p.37.
6. Prepared for the National Housing and Town Planning Council by H.L. Aldridge.
7. As (5), p.40.
8. Supervised by W.R. Jaggard. See also *Country Life*, 20 and 27 November 1920, and Building Research Special Report No.5, 1922.
9. 21 Holders Road, Amesbury, Wiltshire. The roof has since been felted, the windows modernized and porch added.
10. As (5), p.58.
11. As (5), p.54.
12. These steel houses are described in Post-war Building Studies No.1, *House Construction*, HMSO.
13. Jackson, 1970, *The Politics of Architecture*.
14. Boesiger, 1960, *Le Corbusier 1910–60*.
15. *Aujourd'hui*, No.51.
16. *L'Esprit Nouveau*, 1920, editorial.
17. Le Corbusier, 1923, *Vers une Architecture*.
18. Russell, 1981, *Building Systems, Industrialization and Architecture*, p.133, uses the phrase 'a cross between a piece of concrete poetry and a mathematical proof'.
19. Boudon, 1969, *Lived-in Architecture, Pessac Revisited*, p.51.
20. Russell, 1981, *Building Systems, Industrialization and Architecture*, p.85.

21. As (19), p.8.
22. Gropius, 1935, *The New Architecture of the Bauhaus*, p.38.
23. Ibid., p.53.
24. Ibid., p.40.
25. Wagner, 1931, *Das Wachsende Haus*.
26. As (22), p.20.
27. 'Factory-made architecture', *The Architect and Building News*, 15 February 1935.

Chapter 9
1. Walter Gropius was Director of the Bauhaus from its opening in 1919 up to 1928, followed by Hannes Mayer from 1928 to 1930, and Mies van der Rohe from 1930 to its closure in 1933.
2. Naylor, 1985, *The Bauhaus Reassessed*.
3. Passuth, 1985, *Moholy-Nagy*.
4. Naylor, 1985, *The Bauhaus Reassessed*.
5. Ginzburg, 1924, *Stil'i Epokha*, p.38.
6. March and Steadman, 1974, *The Geometry of the Environment*.
7. Nissen, 1972, *Industrialized Building and Modular Design*.
8. Banham, 1960, *Theory and Design in the First Machine Age*, p.148.
9. As (5), p.80.
10. As (5), p.27.
11. Huber and Steinegger (eds), 1971, *Jean Prouvé, Prefabrication, Structures and Elements*.

Chapter 10
1. White, 1965, *Ministry of Technology, National Building Studies, Special Report 36, Prefabrication, A History of its Development in Britain*, p.122.
2. Ibid., p.139.
3. Walker, 1987, *Great Engineers*, p.115.
4. Even Kocher and Fry's Alumnaire House, Long Island, NY, 1931, relied on steel angles for its structure (Banham, 1969, *The Architecture of the Well-Tempered Environment*, p.168).
5. As (1), p.182.
6. The art of enamelling on iron was discovered in Europe in the mid-eighteenth century. In 1764 a factory in Wurttenberg was producing acid-proof enamelled cast-iron stoves and cooking utensils. In 1799 British Patent 2296 was granted to Samual Hickling of Birmingham for lining hammered or cast-iron articles with vitreous compounds (Gloag and Bridgewater, 1948, *A History*

of Cast Iron Architecture, p.81). Vitreous enamelled metal panels were produced in 1857 by Benjamin Baugh at premises at Bradford Street, Birmingham. These were predominantly decorative or sign panels (Clarke, June 1981, *Sign World Magazine*).

7. Russell, 1981, *Building Systems, Industrialization and Architecture*, p.249.
8. Messrs Crittal produced their first range of standard steel cottage windows in the early 1920s (White, as (1), p.45).
9. An early form of plasterboard was produced in Britain in 1917. This, manufactured by the British Plasterboard Company at Wallasey and known as 'Thistleboard', was a small size board which required plastering. it was not until 1926, after the installation of machines from America, that large sheets of superior board were available in Britain (White, as (1), p.331).
10. Lyall, 1980, *The State of British Architecture*, p.95.
11. As (7), p.299.
12. CLASP, 1961, *The Story of CLASP*.
13. As (10), p.107.

Chapter 11

1. Russell, 1946, *A History of Western Philosophy*.
2. Clayre (ed.), 1977, *Nature and Industrialization*.
3. November 1962, *Architectural Design*.
4. Gropius, 1935, *The New Architecture of the Bauhaus*, p.20.
5. *Metropolis* (1926) by Fritz Lang and *Things to Come* (1936) by Alexander Korda.
6. Pawley, March 1989, *RIBA Journal*.
7. 19 January 1989, by Mike Wigginton.
8. Kipling, *A Truthful Song*.
9. Ruskin, 1853, *The Seven Lamps of Architecture*.
10. Machiavelli, *The Prince*.
11. Russell, 1981, *Building Systems, Industrialization and Architecture*.
12. Wood, 17 August 1989, *The Times*.
13. National Building Studies, 1966, *Special Report 39, Qualitative Studies of Buildings*.
14. Johnson, September 1954, Commentary on the Hunstanton School, *Architectural Review*.
15. Boyne, September 1954, *Architects Journal*.
16. Knevitt, 5 September 1986, 'Ronan Point, Bad workmanship found', *The Times*.
17. In association with D.Y. Davies Associates.

18. Perkin, June 1986, Lakeside Headquarters, in *Concrete Quarterly*, 149, p.16.
19. National and Economic Development Office, 1985, *Strategy for Construction Research and Development*, p.17.
20. Saint, 1987, *Towards a Social Architecture*, p.12.
21. Ibid., p.11.
22. Dannatt, October 1987, Edwin Maxwell Fry, *The Architect*.
23. As (20), p.230.
24. July 1988, *Cladding*, Architects Journal Focus.
25. December 1978, *East Anglia Arts*, Architectural Review.
26. Stainless steel was first developed in Sheffield in 1913 by Henry Brearley.
27. Rowe, 1976, *Literal and Phenomena Transparency*.
28. Edmund Happold, in Walker, 1987, *Great Engineers*: 'Is there a separate design approach whose roots are not dependent on visual precedents? I am referring to engineering design as a technological idea, with its own aesthetic'.
29. Peter Ackroyd, 6 April 1989, 'In love with words', *The Times*.

INDEX